Table of Contents

17

Chapter 1: Introduction to Windows 11

1.1. The Evolution of Windows: A Brief History

Windows 11 represents the latest evolution in Microsoft's long history of operating systems. To truly understand the significance of Windows 11, it's essential to take a brief journey through the history of Windows.

Early Windows Versions

The journey begins with Windows 1.0, released in 1985. It was a graphical user interface (GUI) shell for MS-DOS and introduced the concept of overlapping windows, icons, and menus. Windows 2.0 followed, introducing features like desktop icons and improved graphics.

Windows 3.0, released in 1990, was a significant milestone. It brought true multitasking, enhanced graphics, and support for more applications. Windows 3.1 and Windows 3.11 (Workgroups) further refined the experience.

The Windows 95 Era

Windows 95, released in—you guessed it—1995, was a game-changer. It introduced the iconic Start menu, taskbar, and the 32-bit architecture. Plug and Play hardware support made life easier for users.

The Windows NT Lineage

Windows NT, initially released in 1993, was the foundation for Windows 2000, XP, Vista, 7, 8, and 10. This lineage brought a robust and stable platform for businesses and power users.

Windows XP: A Fan Favorite

Windows XP, released in 2001, became a fan favorite. Its polished interface and improved stability made it a long-lasting choice for many users.

The Windows 7 and 8 Era

Windows 7 (2009) and Windows 8 (2012) brought significant changes, with Windows 7 focusing on refining the Windows experience, and Windows 8 introducing a touch-centric interface.

Windows 10: A Step Towards Convergence

Windows 10, launched in 2015, aimed to unify the Windows ecosystem across devices. It introduced features like the Cortana virtual assistant, the Edge browser, and a universal app platform.

Enter Windows 11

And now, we arrive at Windows 11. Released in 2021, Windows 11 builds upon the foundation of Windows 10 while introducing a refreshed user interface, new features, and enhanced performance. It's designed to provide a modern and efficient computing experience.

In this book, we will explore the ins and outs of Windows 11, from its user interface to advanced customization, security, and productivity features. Whether you're a new user or upgrading from a previous version, this book will help you master Windows 11 and make the most of your computing experience. Let's dive in!

1.2. Overview of Windows 11: Key Features and Enhancements

Windows 11 brings a host of key features and enhancements that make it a notable upgrade from its predecessor, Windows 10. In this section, we'll delve into the standout features and improvements that define Windows 11.

Redesigned Start Menu and Taskbar

One of the most noticeable changes in Windows 11 is the redesigned Start Menu and Taskbar. The Start Menu is now centered, providing a cleaner and more modern look. Live Tiles are replaced with static icons for a streamlined appearance. The Taskbar is also centered by default but can be moved to the left if you prefer the classic alignment.

```
To customize the Taskbar position, right-click on it, go to "Taskbar settings
," and choose your preferred alignment under "Taskbar alignment."
```

Snap Layouts and Snap Groups

Windows 11 introduces Snap Layouts and Snap Groups, making multitasking more efficient. Snap Layouts allow you to easily arrange open windows into various layouts, such as side by side or in a grid. Snap Groups help you organize and switch between groups of apps and windows.

```
To use Snap Layouts, drag a window to the screen's edge, and it will snap int
o a suggested layout. To create a Snap Group, open multiple apps, right-click
on a taskbar group, and select "Group."
```

Widgets for Quick Information

Widgets are a new addition to Windows 11, providing at-a-glance information such as weather, news, calendar events, and more. You can access widgets by clicking the Widgets button on the Taskbar.

To customize widgets, click the Widgets button, then click the three dots at the top of the widgets panel and select "Add widgets" to choose the ones you want to see.

Enhanced Virtual Desktops

Virtual Desktops have been enhanced in Windows 11. You can now customize each desktop with different wallpapers and apps. It's an excellent way to organize your workspaces for different tasks or projects.

To create a new Virtual Desktop, press Win + Tab, then click "New Desktop" at the top. To move windows between desktops, drag them to the desired desktop in the Task View.

Redesigned Microsoft Store

The Microsoft Store has undergone a significant redesign, making it more user-friendly and efficient. It offers a wider range of apps, including support for Android apps, and allows developers more flexibility in publishing their software.

Explore the new Microsoft Store by clicking the Microsoft Store icon on your Taskbar. You'll find a refreshed interface and a wider selection of apps.

Gaming Enhancements

For gamers, Windows 11 brings several enhancements, including DirectX 12 Ultimate support, Auto HDR for compatible games, and integration with Xbox Game Pass.

To enable Auto HDR, make sure your hardware supports it, and then enable it in the Windows settings under "Gaming" > "Xbox Game Pass."

These are just a few of the key features and improvements in Windows 11. As we delve deeper into this book, you'll discover even more ways to make the most of your Windows 11 experience.

1.3. Navigating the Windows 11 Interface: Start Menu, Taskbar, and Widgets

Navigating the Windows 11 interface is a fundamental skill for any user. In this section, we'll explore the key elements of the Windows 11 interface, including the Start Menu, Taskbar, and Widgets.

The Centered Start Menu

The Start Menu in Windows 11 has undergone a significant redesign. It's centered on the taskbar, providing a more modern and streamlined appearance. To open the Start Menu, simply click the Windows icon or press the Windows key on your keyboard.

You can also open the Start Menu by pressing Ctrl + Esc or Ctrl + Shift + Esc if your keyboard lacks a Windows key.

Pinned and Recommended Apps

In the Start Menu, you'll find a section for Pinned apps, which are the apps you use most frequently. You can customize this section by right-clicking on an app and selecting "Pin to Start."

Below the Pinned section, you'll find Recommended apps based on your usage patterns. These suggestions can help you discover new apps or quickly access commonly used ones.

The Taskbar

The Taskbar in Windows 11 is typically centered, but you can move it to the left if you prefer the classic alignment. It hosts icons for various functions, including the Start Menu, Task View, Widgets, and system notifications.

To move the Taskbar to the left, right-click on it, go to "Taskbar settings," and change the "Taskbar alignment" to "Left."

Task View and Virtual Desktops

Task View is a feature that allows you to see all your open windows and Virtual Desktops. You can access it by clicking the Task View icon on the Taskbar or by pressing Win + Tab.

To create a new Virtual Desktop, press Win + Tab, then click "New Desktop" at the top. To switch between Virtual Desktops, use the same Win + Tab shortcut.

Widgets for Quick Information

Widgets are a new addition to Windows 11, providing a convenient way to access at-a-glance information. You can open the Widgets panel by clicking the Widgets button on the Taskbar.

To customize widgets, click the Widgets button, then click the three dots at the top of the widgets panel and select "Add widgets" to choose the ones you want to see.

System Notifications

System notifications, including app notifications and system alerts, appear in the lower-right corner of the screen. You can click on them to view details or take action.

To customize notification settings, go to "Settings" > "System" > "Notifications & actions" and adjust the options to your preferences.

These are the core elements of the Windows 11 interface. Familiarizing yourself with them will help you navigate and make the most of your Windows 11 experience. In the following chapters, we'll explore each of these elements in more detail and uncover advanced customization options.

1.4. System Requirements and Installation Guide

Before you can fully embrace Windows 11, it's essential to ensure your computer meets the system requirements and understand how to install it. In this section, we'll cover both aspects to get you started on the right foot.

System Requirements

Windows 11 comes with specific system requirements to ensure a smooth and secure experience. Here are the key hardware requirements:

1. **Processor**: A compatible 64-bit, 1 GHz or faster with at least 2 or more cores.
2. **RAM**: 4 GB or more.
3. **Storage**: 64 GB or more of storage is required.
4. **Graphics Card**: DirectX 12 compatible graphics/WDDM 2.x.
5. **Display**: A high-definition (720p) display that is greater than 9" diagonally, with an aspect ratio of 16:9.
6. **Internet Connection**: Internet connectivity is necessary to perform updates and download apps.

Additionally, Windows 11 introduces the concept of a "PC Health Check" tool that helps you determine whether your PC meets the system requirements. You can download this tool from the official Microsoft website.

Installation Guide

Installing Windows 11 can be a straightforward process if you follow these steps:

1. **Backup Your Data**: Before you start, make sure to back up all your important data to an external drive or cloud storage. The installation process involves formatting your system drive, which will erase all data on it.

2. **Download Windows 11**: You can obtain Windows 11 from official sources, such as the Microsoft website. If you're upgrading from Windows 10, you may be eligible for a free upgrade.

3. **Create Installation Media (Optional)**: If you want to perform a clean installation or upgrade multiple computers, consider creating a bootable USB drive with the Windows 11 installation files using the Media Creation Tool provided by Microsoft.

4. **Insert Installation Media**: If you have a bootable USB drive, insert it into a USB port on your computer. If you downloaded Windows 11, double-click the installation file to begin the upgrade process.

5. **Follow On-Screen Instructions**: The installation process will guide you through selecting your language, region, keyboard layout, and other preferences. Make your selections and click "Next."

6. **Enter Product Key (if required)**: If prompted, enter your Windows 11 product key. This is typically required for clean installations, while upgrades from Windows 10 may not need it.

7. **Choose Installation Type**: Select whether you want to upgrade your existing Windows installation or perform a custom installation (clean install). If you're upgrading from Windows 10, the upgrade option will retain your files and apps.

8. **Partition and Format**: If you're performing a custom installation, you'll need to select a partition for Windows 11. You can format an existing partition or create a new one.

9. **Install Windows 11**: Once you've made your selections, click "Next" and let the installation process run. Your computer will reboot several times during this process.

10. **Set Up Windows**: After the installation is complete, you'll be prompted to set up Windows 11 by creating a user account, choosing settings, and personalizing your desktop.

11. **Windows Update**: Once Windows 11 is installed, it's crucial to run Windows Update to ensure you have the latest drivers and security updates.

12. **Restore Data**: If you backed up your data, now is the time to restore it to your new Windows 11 installation.

Following these steps will help you successfully install Windows 11 on your computer. Ensure that you meet the system requirements and back up your data to avoid any data loss during the installation process.

1.5. Transitioning from Older Windows Versions: What to Expect

If you're upgrading to Windows 11 from an older version of Windows, such as Windows 7, Windows 8, or Windows 10, it's important to understand what to expect during the transition. In this section, we'll cover the key considerations and changes you may encounter when moving to Windows 11.

Compatibility Check

Before upgrading, it's crucial to perform a compatibility check to ensure your hardware meets the system requirements for Windows 11. As mentioned earlier, Windows 11 has specific hardware requirements, and not all older PCs may be eligible for the upgrade. Use the PC Health Check tool provided by Microsoft to determine compatibility.

Start Menu and Taskbar Changes

The Start Menu and Taskbar in Windows 11 have a different appearance and layout compared to older versions. As mentioned earlier, the Start Menu is centered by default, and the Live Tiles found in Windows 10 are replaced with static icons. The Taskbar is also centered, which is a departure from the left-aligned Taskbar in previous versions.

New Features and Enhancements

Windows 11 introduces several new features and enhancements that may enhance your computing experience. Features like Snap Layouts, Snap Groups, and Widgets provide more efficient multitasking and access to information. The redesigned Microsoft Store offers a wider selection of apps, including support for Android apps. These additions can improve productivity and convenience.

System Updates

Windows 11 continues to receive regular updates, including security updates, feature updates, and bug fixes. Microsoft typically provides updates through Windows Update. It's essential to keep your system up to date to ensure security and performance improvements.

Transitioning Your Data

When upgrading to Windows 11, you can choose to retain your files and apps (if upgrading from Windows 10) or perform a clean installation. If you opt for a clean installation, make sure to back up your data before formatting your system drive.

Software Compatibility

While Windows 11 is designed to be compatible with most Windows 10 software, some older or specialized applications may require updates or compatibility mode to function correctly. Check with software vendors for Windows 11 compatibility information.

Customization Options

Windows 11 offers various customization options to personalize your desktop and user experience. You can adjust settings related to the Taskbar, Start Menu, desktop backgrounds, themes, and more to tailor Windows 11 to your preferences.

Support and Resources

As with any new operating system, it's essential to have access to support and resources. Microsoft provides official documentation, forums, and customer support channels to assist users with Windows 11-related queries and issues. Additionally, there are online communities and third-party resources that can be valuable for troubleshooting and learning about Windows 11.

In summary, transitioning from older Windows versions to Windows 11 can bring exciting changes and enhancements to your computing experience. Ensure your hardware is compatible, back up your data, and take advantage of the new features and customization options available in Windows 11. With a smooth transition, you can enjoy the benefits of the latest Windows operating system.

Chapter 2: Setting Up Your Windows 11 Environment

2.1. Personalizing Your Desktop: Backgrounds, Themes, and Layouts

Customizing your Windows 11 desktop is a great way to make your computer feel like your own. In this section, we'll explore how to personalize your desktop with backgrounds, themes, and layouts to create a workspace that suits your style and preferences.

Setting Your Desktop Background

The desktop background, also known as wallpaper, is the image that appears on your desktop. Windows 11 offers several options for setting and customizing your desktop background:

1. **Choose from Predefined Wallpapers**: Windows 11 comes with a collection of predefined wallpapers. To set one of these wallpapers as your background, right-click on the desktop, select "Personalize," and then go to the "Background" section. Choose a wallpaper from the list or click "Browse" to select your own image.

2. **Use Your Own Image**: If you have a favorite image that you'd like to use as your background, you can easily do so. In the "Background" section of the "Personalize" settings, click "Browse" to locate and select your image file.

3. **Slideshow**: You can set your desktop background to change automatically by creating a slideshow. Choose multiple images in the "Background" settings, and Windows will cycle through them at specified intervals.

4. **Solid Color**: If you prefer a simple, solid color background, you can choose a color from the "Background" settings.

To access the "Background" settings, right-click on the desktop, select "Personalize," and then click on "Background."

Applying Themes

Themes in Windows 11 are collections of settings that include background images, colors, sounds, and more. They allow you to quickly change the overall look and feel of your desktop. Here's how to apply a theme:

1. **Select a Theme**: To choose a theme, right-click on the desktop, select "Personalize," and then go to the "Themes" section. Click on a theme to apply it.

2. **Customize Themes**: You can further customize themes by clicking on "Customize" under the selected theme. This allows you to adjust colors, sounds, and other elements to match your preferences.

Taskbar and Start Menu Layouts

Windows 11 offers flexibility in customizing the layout of your Taskbar and Start Menu. You can change the alignment and appearance of these elements to suit your preferences.

1. **Taskbar Alignment**: By default, the Taskbar is centered in Windows 11. If you prefer the classic left-aligned Taskbar, you can change it in the Taskbar settings. Right-click on the Taskbar, select "Taskbar settings," and change the "Taskbar alignment" to "Left."

2. **Start Menu Layout**: You can customize the Start Menu by right-clicking on it and selecting "Taskbar settings." From there, you can choose to hide or show app names, change the icon size, and more.

Dark Mode and Light Mode

Windows 11 offers both Dark Mode and Light Mode, allowing you to choose between a dark or light color scheme for your interface. To switch between these modes, go to "Settings" > "Personalization" > "Colors" and choose your preferred mode.

Personalizing your Windows 11 desktop with backgrounds, themes, and layouts can make your computer feel more inviting and comfortable to use. Experiment with different options to find the combination that suits your style and enhances your productivity.

2.2. Configuring System Settings for Optimal Performance

To ensure your Windows 11 environment runs smoothly and efficiently, it's essential to configure system settings for optimal performance. In this section, we'll explore various settings and tweaks that can help you achieve the best performance on your computer.

Power Plan Settings

Windows 11 offers different power plans that allow you to balance performance and energy efficiency. You can access power plan settings as follows:

1. **Access Power & Sleep Settings**: Go to "Settings" > "System" > "Power & sleep."

2. **Choose a Power Plan**: Under "Power & sleep," click on "Additional power settings." Here, you can choose from predefined power plans like "Balanced," "High performance," and "Power saver."

    – **Balanced**: This plan balances performance and energy conservation. It's suitable for most users.

    – **High Performance**: This plan prioritizes maximum performance but consumes more power and may result in reduced battery life on laptops.

- **Power Saver**: This plan conserves energy and is ideal for extending battery life on laptops.

Select the power plan that best suits your needs. If you want to customize the plan further, click on "Change plan settings" next to your selected plan.

Visual Effects Settings

Windows 11 offers visual effects that enhance the user interface, but these effects can consume system resources. You can adjust these settings for optimal performance:

1. **Access Visual Effects Settings**: Right-click on "This PC" or "My Computer" and select "Properties." Click on "Advanced system settings" in the left sidebar, then click the "Settings" button under the "Performance" section.

2. **Choose Performance Options**: In the "Performance Options" window, you can choose between "Let Windows choose what's best for my computer" and "Adjust for best performance." Selecting the latter will disable most visual effects for better performance. You can also customize specific visual effects under the "Custom" tab.

Startup Programs

Managing startup programs is crucial for a faster boot time and improved system performance. Here's how to control which programs start with Windows:

1. **Access Startup Programs**: Right-click on the Taskbar and select "Task Manager." Go to the "Startup" tab to view a list of programs that start with Windows.

2. **Disable Unnecessary Startup Programs**: Identify programs you don't need to start with Windows and disable them. Right-click on a program and select "Disable."

   - Be cautious when disabling startup programs, as some may be essential for your system or desired functionality. Research unfamiliar programs before disabling them.

Disk Cleanup

Over time, your computer accumulates temporary files and other unnecessary data that can slow down your system. You can use Disk Cleanup to remove these files:

1. **Access Disk Cleanup**: Press the Windows key and type "Disk Cleanup," then select the "Disk Cleanup" app.

2. **Select Drive and Files to Clean**: Choose the drive you want to clean (typically your system drive, labeled "C:") and click "OK." Disk Cleanup will scan for unnecessary files.

3. **Select File Types**: In the Disk Cleanup window, you can select which types of files to delete. Common options include "Temporary files," "Recycle Bin," and "System error memory dump files." Check the boxes for the files you want to remove.

4. **Start Cleanup**: Click "OK" to start the cleanup process. Disk Cleanup will free up space by removing the selected files.

Disk Optimization

Regularly optimizing your computer's storage drive (HDD or SSD) can help maintain performance. Here's how to optimize your drive:

1. **Access Drive Optimization**: Press the Windows key and type "Defragment and Optimize Drives," then select the app.

2. **Select Drive**: In the "Optimize Drives" window, select the drive you want to optimize (typically your system drive, labeled "C:") and click "Optimize."

Optimizing your drive reorganizes data to improve access times, especially on traditional hard drives (HDDs).

Adjusting Visual Effects and Animations

Windows 11 includes various animations and visual effects that enhance the user interface but can consume system resources. You can adjust these settings for better performance:

1. **Access Visual Effects Settings**: Right-click on "This PC" or "My Computer" and select "Properties." Click on "Advanced system settings" in the left sidebar, then click the "Settings" button under the "Performance" section.

2. **Customize Visual Effects**: In the "Performance Options" window, you can choose between "Let Windows choose what's best for my computer" and "Adjust for best performance." Selecting the latter will disable most visual effects for better performance. You can also customize specific visual effects under the "Custom" tab.

Uninstalling Unused Software

Removing unused or unnecessary software can free up storage space and potentially improve system performance. Here's how to uninstall programs:

1. **Access Apps & Features**: Go to "Settings" > "Apps" > "Apps & features."

2. **Uninstall Software**: Scroll through the list of installed apps and select the one you want to uninstall. Click "Uninstall" to remove the program from your computer.

Regularly reviewing and optimizing your system settings can significantly impact your Windows 11 computer's performance. By following these steps and making necessary adjustments, you can ensure that your computer runs smoothly and efficiently.

2.3. Setting Up User Accounts and Family Safety Features

Setting up user accounts and configuring family safety features in Windows 11 is essential to personalize your experience and ensure a safe computing environment for yourself and your family members. In this section, we'll explore how to create and manage user accounts and use family safety features.

Creating a User Account

Windows 11 allows you to create multiple user accounts, each with its own settings and permissions. To create a new user account, follow these steps:

1. **Access User Accounts Settings**: Press the Windows key and type "User Accounts," then select "User Accounts" from the search results.

2. **Manage Accounts**: In the User Accounts window, click on "Manage another account."

3. **Add a New Account**: Click on "Add a new user in PC settings." This will open the Settings app.

4. **Add a Family Member or Other Users**: You can choose to add a family member (for family safety features) or other users (for standard accounts). Follow the on-screen instructions to complete the account creation process.

Configuring Account Type and Permissions

When creating a user account, you can choose the account type and set permissions accordingly:

*   **Administrator**: An administrator account has full control over the computer, including installing software, changing system settings, and managing other user accounts. Use this type of account carefully.

*   **Standard User**: A standard user account is more restricted and can't make significant system changes. It's suitable for everyday use to prevent accidental system alterations.

*   **Child Account**: If you're setting up an account for a child, you can create a child account with additional safety features and parental controls.

Managing Family Safety Features

Windows 11 offers robust family safety features to help parents monitor and control their children's online activities. Here's how to set up and manage family safety settings:

1. **Access Family Safety Settings**: Press the Windows key and type "Family Safety Settings," then select "Family Safety Settings" from the search results.

2. **Add a Child**: To monitor a child's activities, you need to add them to your family group. Click on "Add a child" and follow the instructions to create a child account.

3. **Manage Family Settings Online**: You can also manage family settings online through the Microsoft Family Safety website. This allows you to set screen time limits, review activity reports, and control app and game access for your child's account.

Screen Time Limits

You can set screen time limits to help manage how much time your child spends on their Windows 11 device. To configure screen time limits:

1. **Access Family Safety Settings**: Press the Windows key and type "Family Safety Settings," then select "Family Safety Settings" from the search results.

2. **Select Your Child's Account**: Under "Your family," click on your child's account.

3. **Set Screen Time**: Under "Screen time," click "Set limits for apps and games." From here, you can set daily limits for specific apps and games.

App and Game Restrictions

You can control which apps and games your child can access on their Windows 11 device. To configure app and game restrictions:

1. **Access Family Safety Settings**: Press the Windows key and type "Family Safety Settings," then select "Family Safety Settings" from the search results.

2. **Select Your Child's Account**: Under "Your family," click on your child's account.

3. **Manage App and Game Restrictions**: Under "Content restrictions," click "Apps, games & media." Here, you can set age-appropriate app and game limits.

4. **Block Inappropriate Apps and Games**: You can also block specific apps and games that you don't want your child to access.

Configuring user accounts and family safety settings in Windows 11 allows you to create a customized and secure computing environment for yourself and your family members. Whether you're setting up individual accounts or managing family safety features, these settings help you personalize your Windows experience and ensure online safety for all users.

2.4. Accessibility Features in Windows 11

Windows 11 places a strong emphasis on accessibility, ensuring that individuals with diverse needs can use the operating system effectively. In this section, we'll explore the accessibility features available in Windows 11 and how they can be configured to enhance usability.

To access accessibility features and settings in Windows 11, you can follow these steps:

1. **Open Settings**: Click on the "Start" button, then click on the gear-shaped "Settings" icon.

2. **Navigate to Accessibility**: In the Settings window, click on "Accessibility" in the left sidebar. This will take you to the Ease of Access settings.

Visual Accessibility Features

1. Magnifier

The Magnifier tool enlarges portions of the screen, making content more accessible for individuals with visual impairments or those who require a closer view.

- **Enabling Magnifier**: In the Ease of Access settings, click on "Magnifier" to configure its settings. You can choose to turn it on and customize zoom levels, tracking options, and other settings.

2. Narrator

Narrator is a screen-reading tool that reads aloud on-screen text, making it useful for visually impaired users. To enable Narrator:

- **Enabling Narrator**: In the Ease of Access settings, click on "Narrator" to configure its settings. You can toggle it on or off and customize voice settings.

3. High Contrast Mode

High Contrast Mode changes the colors and background to improve visibility for individuals with visual impairments or sensitivity to certain color combinations.

- **Enabling High Contrast Mode**: In the Ease of Access settings, click on "High contrast" to choose from predefined high-contrast themes.

Hearing Accessibility Features

1. Closed Captions and Subtitles

Windows 11 provides the ability to enable closed captions and subtitles for videos and audio content.

- **Enabling Closed Captions**: To enable closed captions for videos and audio, go to "Settings" > "Accessibility" > "Closed captions" and turn on the "Closed captions" toggle.

2. Sound Enhancements

For users with hearing impairments, Windows 11 offers various sound enhancements, including mono audio and visual notifications.

- **Mono Audio**: In the "Audio" section of the Ease of Access settings, you can enable mono audio to combine stereo audio channels into a single channel for improved sound clarity.

- **Visual Notifications**: You can also enable visual notifications that provide visual cues for system sounds and events in the "Audio" section of the Ease of Access settings.

Input Accessibility Features

1. On-Screen Keyboard

The on-screen keyboard is a virtual keyboard that can be used with touch devices or when physical keyboards are unavailable.

- **Enabling the On-Screen Keyboard**: In the Ease of Access settings, click on "Keyboard" to enable the on-screen keyboard and customize its appearance and behavior.

Other Accessibility Features

1. Keyboard Shortcuts

Windows 11 offers keyboard shortcuts that can assist individuals with physical disabilities in navigating the operating system more efficiently.

- **Keyboard Shortcut Reference**: You can find a list of keyboard shortcuts in the "Keyboard" section of the Ease of Access settings.

2. Eye Control

For users with limited mobility, Windows 11 includes Eye Control, which allows control of the mouse pointer and interaction with on-screen elements using eye-tracking technology.

- **Enabling Eye Control**: In the Ease of Access settings, click on "Eye Control" to configure eye-tracking settings if you have the compatible hardware.

These accessibility features in Windows 11 aim to make the operating system more inclusive and user-friendly for individuals with various needs. By customizing these features to suit individual requirements, users can have a more accessible and accommodating computing experience.

2.5. Essential Security Settings: Privacy and Data Protection

Ensuring the privacy and security of your data is a fundamental aspect of using any operating system, including Windows 11. In this section, we'll explore essential security settings in Windows 11 that you can configure to protect your privacy and data.

Windows Security

Windows 11 comes equipped with Windows Security, a comprehensive suite of security features to safeguard your computer. You can access Windows Security through the following steps:

1. **Open Settings**: Click on the "Start" button, then click on the gear-shaped "Settings" icon.

2. **Navigate to Windows Security**: In the Settings window, click on "Privacy & Security" in the left sidebar, and then click on "Windows Security."

Antivirus Protection

Windows Security includes built-in antivirus protection powered by Windows Defender Antivirus. It provides real-time protection against viruses, malware, and other threats. Ensure that it's enabled and up to date:

-   **Checking Antivirus Status**: In Windows Security, under "Virus & threat protection," you can check the status of your antivirus protection. Ensure that "Real-time protection" is turned on.

-   **Updating Antivirus Definitions**: Windows Defender Antivirus automatically updates its definitions to detect the latest threats. However, you can also check for updates manually under "Virus & threat protection."

Firewall Settings

The Windows Firewall is a crucial security feature that controls incoming and outgoing network traffic. It helps protect your computer from unauthorized access and network-based attacks.

-   **Configuring Firewall Settings**: In Windows Security, click on "Firewall & network protection" to access firewall settings. Here, you can customize inbound and outbound rules for specific apps and features.

Account Protection

Account protection settings are vital to safeguarding your online accounts and personal information. Windows 11 offers features like Windows Hello and account recovery options.

-   **Setting Up Windows Hello**: If your device supports it, you can set up Windows Hello for biometric authentication (such as fingerprint or facial recognition) to enhance account security.

- **Account Recovery Options**: In the "Account protection" section of Windows Security, you can set up account recovery options, such as a secondary email address or phone number, to regain access to your Microsoft account if needed.

Privacy Settings

Windows 11 allows you to control and customize privacy settings to determine what information and data apps can access. Here are some essential privacy settings:

- **Privacy Dashboard**: Windows 11 provides a Privacy Dashboard that allows you to review and control various privacy settings in one place. You can access it under "Privacy" in Windows Security.

- **App Permissions**: In "App permissions," you can manage permissions for apps, such as access to your camera, microphone, and location.

- **Activity History**: If you use a Microsoft account, you can choose whether to enable or disable activity history tracking, which includes information about your app and browser activity.

Windows Updates

Keeping your operating system up to date is crucial for security. Windows 11 regularly receives updates that include security patches and bug fixes.

- **Checking for Updates**: In Windows Security, click on "Windows Update" to check for and install the latest updates. Ensure that automatic updates are enabled for ongoing protection.

Device Encryption

Windows 11 offers device encryption to protect your data in case your device is lost or stolen. It uses BitLocker technology to encrypt the contents of your device's storage drive.

- **Enabling Device Encryption**: To enable device encryption, go to "Settings" > "Privacy & Security" > "Device encryption" and follow the prompts to encrypt your device.

Secure Boot

Secure Boot is a feature that ensures only trusted software is loaded during the boot process, preventing malware or unauthorized code from running at startup.

- **Checking Secure Boot Status**: In the BIOS or UEFI settings of your computer, you can check the status of Secure Boot. Ensure that it's enabled for enhanced security.

By configuring these essential security settings in Windows 11, you can significantly enhance the protection of your data and privacy. Regularly reviewing and adjusting these settings ensures that your computer remains secure against various threats and vulnerabilities.

Chapter 3: File Management Fundamentals

3.1. Exploring File Explorer: Navigation and Customization

File Explorer is a central tool in Windows 11 that allows you to manage your files and folders efficiently. Understanding how to navigate and customize File Explorer is essential for organizing and accessing your files. In this section, we'll delve into File Explorer's features and how to make the most of them.

Launching File Explorer

You can open File Explorer in several ways:

- **Using the Taskbar**: By default, File Explorer is pinned to the taskbar. Simply click on its icon to open it.

- **Using Keyboard Shortcuts**: Press Win + E on your keyboard to open File Explorer quickly.

- **Using the Start Menu**: Click on the "Start" button, and then select "File Explorer" from the menu.

Understanding the File Explorer Interface

File Explorer's interface consists of several elements that help you navigate and manage files:

1. **Ribbon**: The Ribbon is located at the top of the File Explorer window and contains various tabs with commands for file management. You'll find commands like "Copy," "Paste," "Delete," and "New Folder" here.

2. **Address Bar**: The Address Bar displays the current location (folder or directory) you are in. You can click on it to enter a specific path or address.

3. **Navigation Pane**: The Navigation Pane is on the left side of the window and displays a tree view of your file system, including Quick Access, This PC (your local drives), and network locations.

4. **File List**: The central area of the window displays the contents of the currently selected folder. You can sort, filter, and view your files and folders here.

5. **Preview Pane**: On the right side (optional), you can enable the Preview Pane to see a preview of selected files without opening them.

Navigating Folders

Navigating folders in File Explorer is straightforward:

- **Double-Click**: To enter a folder, simply double-click on its icon in the file list.

- **Back and Forward**: Use the back (left arrow) and forward (right arrow) buttons in the top-left corner of the window to move backward and forward through your navigation history.

- **Address Bar**: You can also use the Address Bar to navigate. Click on it, type the path or address, and press Enter.

Customizing File Explorer

You can customize File Explorer to suit your preferences and workflow. Here are some customization options:

1. **Changing the View**: In the Ribbon's "View" tab, you can choose from different view options, such as "Extra large icons," "Details," or "List," to change how files and folders are displayed.

2. **Customizing the Quick Access**: You can pin frequently used folders and locations to Quick Access in the Navigation Pane for quick access.

3. **Sorting and Grouping**: In the file list, click on the column headers to sort files and folders by name, date, size, or type. You can also group them for better organization.

4. **Changing Folder Options**: Go to the "View" tab in the Ribbon and click on "Options." In the Folder Options window, you can customize settings like displaying hidden files, enabling file extensions, and more.

5. **Setting Default Folder Options**: In "Folder Options," you can set default options for how File Explorer behaves, such as whether it opens to "This PC" or "Quick Access" when launched.

6. **Customizing the Quick Access Toolbar**: You can add frequently used commands to the Quick Access Toolbar for quick access. Right-click on a command in the Ribbon and select "Add to Quick Access Toolbar."

7. **Pin to Taskbar**: If you use File Explorer extensively, you can pin it to the taskbar for one-click access.

File Explorer is a powerful tool for managing your files and folders in Windows 11. By understanding its interface, navigation, and customization options, you can streamline your file management tasks and work more efficiently. Explore the various features and settings to tailor File Explorer to your specific needs and preferences.

3.2. Organizing Files and Folders: Best Practices

Efficiently organizing your files and folders is essential for easy access and effective file management in Windows 11. In this section, we'll explore best practices for structuring your file system, naming conventions, and tips to keep your files organized.

Folder Structure

A well-organized folder structure is the foundation of effective file management. Consider the following tips when structuring your folders:

1. **Keep It Simple**: Avoid excessive nesting of folders. A deep hierarchy can make it challenging to find files quickly. Aim for a balance between organization and simplicity.

2. **Use Descriptive Folder Names**: Choose folder names that clearly describe their contents. This makes it easier to locate files later.

3. **Categorize by Purpose**: Group related files together. For example, you might have separate folders for work, personal, and projects.

4. **Avoid Overcrowding**: Don't put too many files in a single folder. If a folder becomes cluttered, consider creating subfolders to further categorize files.

5. **Utilize Default Folders**: Windows 11 provides default folders like Documents, Pictures, Music, and Videos. Use these as intended to maintain a clear structure.

6. **Date-Based Folders**: Consider using date-based folders for organizing files chronologically. For example, you can create folders with the format "YYYY-MM-DD" for specific events or projects.

File Naming Conventions

Consistent and descriptive file names are crucial for quickly identifying the content of a file. Follow these naming conventions:

1. **Use Clear and Concise Names**: Keep file names short and meaningful. Avoid overly long or cryptic names.

2. **Include Dates**: If relevant, include dates in file names. This is particularly useful for version control or organizing files by date.

3. **Avoid Special Characters**: Use letters, numbers, and basic punctuation in file names. Avoid special characters or symbols that may cause compatibility issues.

4. **Use Underscores or Hyphens**: When separating words in a file name, consider using underscores (_) or hyphens (-) instead of spaces for better compatibility.

5. **Version Numbers**: If you frequently update files, consider including version numbers in file names (e.g., "Project_Report_V1.docx").

6. **Consistent Capitalization**: Choose a consistent capitalization style (e.g., camelCase, TitleCase, or lowercase) and stick to it.

File Metadata

File metadata, such as tags and properties, can be valuable for organizing and searching for files. Windows 11 allows you to add metadata to files:

1. **Tags**: You can add tags to files to categorize them. Right-click on a file, select "Properties," and go to the "Details" tab to add tags.

2. **File Properties**: In the "Details" tab of file properties, you can enter additional information like author, title, and comments. This can be useful for document management.

Regular Cleanup

Maintaining your file system requires periodic cleanup:

1. **Delete Unnecessary Files**: Regularly go through your files and delete any that are no longer needed. This reduces clutter and frees up storage space.

2. **Move or Archive Old Files**: For files you want to keep but don't need to access frequently, consider moving them to an archive folder or an external drive.

3. **Empty the Recycle Bin**: After deleting files, remember to empty the Recycle Bin to free up disk space.

Backups

Always maintain backups of important files to protect against data loss. Use Windows 11's built-in backup tools or third-party backup solutions to regularly back up your files to an external drive or cloud storage.

Search Functionality

Windows 11 offers powerful search capabilities. Use the search bar in File Explorer to quickly locate files by name, content, date, or metadata. Familiarize yourself with search operators to refine your searches further.

By following these best practices for organizing files and folders, you can maintain a tidy and efficient file system in Windows 11. This not only enhances productivity but also ensures that your valuable data is easily accessible and well-protected.

3.3. Using OneDrive for Cloud Storage and Synchronization

OneDrive is Microsoft's cloud storage and synchronization service integrated into Windows 11. It allows you to store files and folders in the cloud, access them from any device with an internet connection, and keep your files synchronized across all your devices. In this section, we'll explore how to use OneDrive effectively for file storage and synchronization.

Setting Up OneDrive

To get started with OneDrive on Windows 11, follow these steps:

1. **Sign In**: Sign in to Windows 11 with your Microsoft account. If you don't have one, you can create a free Microsoft account.

2. **Enable OneDrive**: OneDrive is often pre-installed on Windows 11. If not, you can download and install it from the Microsoft website.

3. **Sign In to OneDrive**: Launch the OneDrive app and sign in with your Microsoft account credentials. This will link your Windows profile to OneDrive.

4. **Choose Folders to Sync**: During setup, you can select which folders and files from your OneDrive you want to sync with your local device. You can choose to sync everything or specific folders.

Uploading Files to OneDrive

To upload files and folders to OneDrive:

1. **Drag and Drop**: Simply drag files or folders from your computer and drop them into the OneDrive folder in File Explorer. They will be uploaded to your OneDrive cloud storage.

2. **Use the OneDrive App**: You can also upload files using the OneDrive app by clicking the "Upload" button and selecting files or folders to upload.

Accessing Files from Anywhere

One of the key benefits of OneDrive is the ability to access your files from anywhere with an internet connection. You can do this through:

1. **OneDrive Web**: Visit the OneDrive website (onedrive.live.com) and sign in with your Microsoft account to access your files online.

2. **OneDrive Mobile App**: Install the OneDrive mobile app on your iOS or Android device to access your files on the go.

Synchronizing Files Across Devices

OneDrive keeps your files synchronized across all your devices. Here's how it works:

1. **Changes Made on One Device**: When you edit or add files on one device, those changes are automatically synchronized to your other devices with OneDrive.

2. **Access Files Offline**: OneDrive allows you to access certain files and folders offline. You can choose which files to keep offline in the OneDrive app settings.

3. **Collaboration**: OneDrive makes it easy to collaborate on documents with others. You can share files and folders with specific people and set permissions for viewing or editing.

Version History and Recovery

OneDrive also provides version history for your files, which is useful in case you need to recover a previous version:

1. **Version History**: Right-click on a file in OneDrive, select "Version history," and you can view and restore previous versions of that file.

2. **Deleted Files**: OneDrive has a "Recycle Bin" where deleted files are temporarily stored. You can recover deleted files from here within a certain timeframe.

Storage Plans

OneDrive offers a certain amount of free storage, but if you need more space, you can subscribe to a OneDrive storage plan. These plans provide additional storage capacity and other premium features.

Troubleshooting Sync Issues

While OneDrive generally works smoothly, you may encounter sync issues. If you do, you can:

- **Check Internet Connection**: Ensure that you have a stable internet connection.

- **Check OneDrive Status**: Microsoft maintains a status page for OneDrive where you can check if there are any ongoing service issues.

- **Restart OneDrive**: Sometimes, simply restarting the OneDrive app or your computer can resolve sync problems.

OneDrive is a powerful tool for cloud storage and synchronization in Windows 11. By setting it up and using it effectively, you can ensure that your files are accessible and up-to-date across all your devices while also benefiting from version history and easy collaboration options.

3.4. Mastering Search: Finding Files Efficiently

Windows 11 provides powerful search capabilities that make it easy to locate files and folders on your computer. Whether you have a large collection of documents or just a few files, knowing how to use search effectively can save you time and frustration. In this section, we'll explore how to master file search in Windows 11.

Using the Search Bar

The search bar in Windows 11 is located on the taskbar. It's a central place where you can initiate searches. Here's how to use it:

1. **Click the Search Icon**: Click on the magnifying glass icon or simply press the Win + S keyboard shortcut to open the search bar.

2. **Start Typing**: Begin typing your search query. As you type, Windows will start displaying relevant search results.

3. **Filter Results**: You can filter results by selecting the type of content you're looking for, such as apps, documents, settings, or more. These filters appear above the search results.

File Content Search

Windows 11 includes the ability to search within the content of files, not just file names. This is especially useful for finding specific text within documents. Here's how to do it:

1. **Enter Your Query**: In the search bar, enter your query. For example, if you're looking for a document containing the word "project," type "project."

2. **Filter by "All"**: Make sure the search filter is set to "All" to search for content within files.

3. **Review Results**: Windows will display a list of files containing the search term. You can click on a file to open it directly.

Advanced Search Operators

Windows 11 supports various search operators to help you refine your searches further. Here are some examples:

- **AND Operator**: Use "AND" to search for files containing both terms. For example, "project AND budget" will find files that contain both "project" and "budget."

- **OR Operator**: Use "OR" to search for files containing either of the terms. For example, "presentation OR report" will find files containing either "presentation" or "report."

- **NOT Operator**: Use "NOT" to exclude specific terms from your search. For example, "meeting NOT minutes" will find files containing "meeting" but not "minutes."

- **Quotation Marks**: Use quotation marks to search for an exact phrase. For example, "financial report" will find files containing the phrase "financial report."

Windows 11 also provides advanced search filters to narrow down your search results:

- **Date Modified**: You can filter results by the date when files were last modified, making it useful for finding recent files.

- **File Type**: You can specify the file type you're looking for, such as documents, images, or videos.

- **Size**: You can filter files by their size, which is helpful when searching for large or small files.

Indexing Options

Windows relies on an index to provide fast search results. If you're not getting the results you expect, you can check and customize indexing options:

1. **Open Indexing Options**: Type "Indexing Options" in the search bar and open the corresponding settings.

2. **Modify Index Locations**: You can add or remove folders from the indexing locations. Adding a folder ensures its contents are searchable.

3. **Rebuild the Index**: If you encounter issues with search, you can rebuild the index to refresh it. This process may take some time.

By mastering search in Windows 11 and using advanced operators and filters, you can quickly find the files you need, whether they're located in your Documents folder, on an external drive, or within the content of documents themselves. Effective search is a time-saving skill that enhances your productivity on the computer.

3.5. Backup and Restore Options: Keeping Your Data Safe

Backing up your data is crucial to safeguarding it against accidental loss, hardware failures, or other unforeseen events. Windows 11 offers various backup and restore options to ensure that your important files are protected. In this section, we'll explore how to use these options effectively.

File History

File History is a built-in backup feature in Windows 11 that allows you to automatically back up your files to an external drive or network location. Here's how to set it up:

1. **Connect an External Drive**: To begin, connect an external hard drive or configure a network location for storing your backups.

2. **Enable File History**:

   - Click on the "Start" button, then go to "Settings" > "Privacy & Security" > "Backup."
   - Under "Backup using File History," click on "Add a drive" and select your external drive or network location.

3. **Configure Backup Settings**: You can customize backup settings like the frequency of backups and how long to keep versions of files.

4. **Start Backing Up**: Once configured, File History will automatically back up your files at the chosen intervals.

System Restore

System Restore is a feature that allows you to revert your Windows system files and settings to an earlier point in time, known as a restore point. It doesn't affect your personal files, but it can help resolve system issues. Here's how to use it:

1. **Create a Restore Point**:

   - Type "Create a restore point" in the search bar and open the corresponding settings.
   - In the "System Properties" window, go to the "System Restore" tab and click on "Create."

2. **Follow the Wizard**: Give your restore point a descriptive name and follow the wizard to create it.

3. **Restore Your System**:

   - If you encounter a system issue, type "Create a restore point" in the search bar again and select it.
   - In the "System Properties" window, click on "System Restore" and follow the wizard to restore your system to the chosen restore point.

Backup and Restore Settings

Windows 11 provides additional backup and restore settings that you can access through the "Settings" app:

1. **Backup**: Go to "Settings" > "Privacy & Security" > "Backup" to configure backup settings. You can back up files, settings, and apps to an external drive.

2. **Recovery**: Under "Settings" > "Update & Security" > "Recovery," you can access options for resetting your PC, advanced startup, and reinstalling Windows.

Third-Party Backup Solutions

While Windows 11 offers built-in backup options, you can also explore third-party backup solutions for more advanced features and flexibility. Popular backup software like Acronis True Image, EaseUS Todo Backup, and Macrium Reflect offer comprehensive backup and recovery capabilities.

Cloud Backup

Consider using cloud backup services like Microsoft OneDrive, Google Drive, or Dropbox for storing important files. These services offer secure cloud storage and synchronization, ensuring that your data is accessible from any device with an internet connection.

Regular Backup Routine

To ensure the safety of your data, it's essential to establish a regular backup routine. Here are some best practices:

- **Set Automatic Backups**: Schedule regular automatic backups using built-in tools like File History.

- **Multiple Copies**: Keep multiple copies of important files in different locations, such as an external drive and cloud storage.

- **Regular Checkup**: Periodically verify that your backups are working correctly and that you can restore files if needed.

- **Offsite Backup**: Consider keeping a backup copy of critical data offsite to protect against physical damage or theft.

- **Document Backup Procedures**: If multiple people use the computer, ensure that everyone is aware of the backup procedures and can access backups if necessary.

By implementing these backup and restore options and establishing a routine for data protection, you can significantly reduce the risk of data loss and maintain the integrity of your files and settings in Windows 11.

Chapter 4: Installing and Managing Applications

4.1. Using the Microsoft Store: Finding and Installing Apps

The Microsoft Store is the official marketplace for Windows 11 apps and offers a wide range of applications, both free and paid, that you can install on your computer. In this section, we'll explore how to use the Microsoft Store to find and install apps efficiently.

Accessing the Microsoft Store

To access the Microsoft Store, follow these steps:

1. **Open the Start Menu**: Click on the "Start" button located in the taskbar.

2. **Launch Microsoft Store**: You can find the Microsoft Store icon in the Start Menu. Click on it to open the store.

Browsing and Searching for Apps

Once you're in the Microsoft Store, you can find apps in several ways:

1. **Browse Categories**: The store offers various categories such as Apps, Games, Entertainment, and Productivity. Click on a category to explore apps within that category.

2. **Search**: Use the search bar located at the top right corner of the Microsoft Store to search for specific apps or keywords. As you type, the store will suggest relevant results.

3. **Top Charts**: Check out the "Top Charts" section to see the most popular apps and games in different categories.

4. **Collections**: Microsoft Store often curates collections of apps based on themes, seasons, or special occasions. Explore these collections for app recommendations.

App Details and Reviews

Before installing an app, it's a good practice to review its details and read user reviews:

1. **App Details**: When you click on an app, you'll be taken to its details page. Here, you can find a description, screenshots, system requirements, and other relevant information about the app.

2. **Reviews and Ratings**: Scroll down on the app's details page to read user reviews and see its rating. This can help you gauge the quality and reliability of the app.

Installing Apps

To install an app from the Microsoft Store:

1. **App Details Page**: On the app's details page, click the "Install" or "Get" button. If it's a paid app, you'll be prompted to purchase it before installing.

2. **Microsoft Account**: If you're not already signed in with your Microsoft account, you'll be asked to sign in or create one. This account is used to manage your app installations.

3. **Confirmation**: Confirm the installation by clicking "Install" again. The app will begin downloading and installing on your computer.

4. **Start Menu**: After installation, you can find the app in your Start Menu. Click on it to launch the app.

Updating Apps

Apps from the Microsoft Store are automatically updated by default. However, you can manually check for updates:

1. **Microsoft Store**: Open the Microsoft Store, click on the three horizontal dots (ellipsis) in the top-right corner, and select "Downloads and updates." Here, you can see available updates and click "Get updates" to install them.

Managing Installed Apps

To manage the apps you've installed:

1. **Uninstalling Apps**: Right-click on an app in the Start Menu or Apps list and select "Uninstall." Alternatively, you can go to "Settings" > "Apps" > "Apps & features" to uninstall apps.

2. **App Settings**: Some apps have their settings accessible through the Settings app. You can customize app-specific settings there.

3. **App Permissions**: Under "Settings" > "Privacy," you can manage app permissions, including camera, microphone, location, and more.

4. **App Updates**: As mentioned earlier, you can manually check for app updates in the Microsoft Store.

Troubleshooting Installation Issues

If you encounter issues while installing apps from the Microsoft Store, try the following troubleshooting steps:

- Check your internet connection to ensure it's stable.
- Restart your computer, as this can sometimes resolve installation problems.
- Ensure that your Windows 11 is up to date by installing the latest Windows updates.
- Sign out of the Microsoft Store and sign back in with your Microsoft account.
- Check for any pending system updates, as they may be causing conflicts with app installations.

By using the Microsoft Store, you can easily find, install, and manage a wide variety of apps on your Windows 11 computer. It's a convenient and secure way to enhance the functionality of your system and cater to your specific needs.

4.2. Installing Applications from External Sources

While the Microsoft Store is the primary source for Windows 11 apps, there may be instances where you want to install applications from external sources. These sources could include software downloaded from the internet, installation files on physical media, or networked drives. In this section, we'll explore how to safely install applications from external sources on Windows 11.

Safety Precautions

Before downloading and installing applications from external sources, it's essential to take safety precautions to protect your computer from potential risks:

1. **Verify the Source**: Ensure that you are downloading software from a reputable and trusted source. Avoid downloading applications from unverified websites or suspicious sources.

2. **Check for Authenticity**: Verify that the application you are downloading is the official and unaltered version. Look for digital signatures or checksums provided by the software developer.

3. **Use Antivirus Software**: Keep your antivirus software up to date and run a scan on any downloaded files to check for malware or viruses.

4. **Keep Windows Updated**: Ensure that your Windows 11 operating system is up to date with the latest security patches and updates.

Downloading Installation Files

When you download an application from an external source, it typically comes in the form of an installation file or package. These files often have extensions like .exe, .msi, .zip, or .dmg. Here's how to proceed with installing such applications:

1. **Download the Installation File**: Download the application's installation file from the official website or a trusted source. Save it to a location on your computer where you can easily locate it.

2. **Check System Requirements**: Before installation, review the application's system requirements to ensure that your computer meets the necessary specifications.

To install an application from an external source:

1. **Locate the Installation File**: Navigate to the folder where you saved the installation file.

2. **Run the Installer**: Double-click on the installation file. Windows will typically display a User Account Control (UAC) prompt to confirm the installation. Click "Yes" to proceed.

3. **Follow Installation Wizard**: The installation process often involves a wizard that guides you through the setup. Read and accept the software's license agreement, choose installation options (if applicable), and select the installation directory.

4. **Installation**: Click "Install" or a similar button to initiate the installation. The progress bar will indicate the installation status.

5. **Completing the Installation**: Once the installation is complete, you may be prompted to launch the application immediately. You can choose to do so or exit the installer.

Uninstalling External Applications

To uninstall applications installed from external sources:

1. **Open Settings**: Click on the "Start" button, then go to "Settings."

2. **Go to Apps**: In the "Settings" window, select "Apps."

3. **Select the Application**: Scroll through the list of installed apps and select the application you want to uninstall.

4. **Uninstall**: Click the "Uninstall" button associated with the selected application. Confirm the uninstallation when prompted.

Updating External Applications

Applications installed from external sources may not update automatically like those from the Microsoft Store. To update them, you'll need to:

1. **Visit the Official Website**: Go to the official website of the application's developer to check for updates.

2. **Download and Install Updates**: If updates are available, download the latest version and follow the installation instructions as you did during the initial installation.

3. **Check for In-App Updates**: Some applications have built-in update checks. Check the application's settings or menu for an update option.

By following these guidelines and practicing caution, you can safely install applications from external sources on Windows 11. It's essential to ensure that the sources are trustworthy, and you verify the authenticity of the software to maintain the security and stability of your computer.

4.3. Managing Installed Applications: Updates and Removal

Once you have installed applications on your Windows 11 computer, it's important to manage them effectively. This includes keeping them up to date with the latest versions and, when necessary, removing unwanted or obsolete applications. In this section, we'll explore how to manage installed applications, including updating and uninstalling them.

Updating Applications

Keeping your installed applications up to date is crucial for security, stability, and accessing new features or bug fixes. Here's how to update your applications:

1. **Using the Microsoft Store**:

    –   Open the Microsoft Store from the Start Menu.
    –   Click on the three horizontal dots (ellipsis) in the top-right corner and select "Downloads and updates."
    –   Click "Get updates" to check for and install available updates for Microsoft Store apps.

2. **Using Application Settings**:

    –   Some applications have built-in update checks. Open the application, and look for an "Update" or "Check for Updates" option in the settings menu.

3. **Third-Party Software Updaters**:

    –   Some applications provide automatic update mechanisms. For instance, web browsers like Google Chrome and Mozilla Firefox often update themselves in the background.

4. **Manual Updates**:

    –   If an application doesn't have an automatic update feature, visit the official website of the software developer to download and install the latest version manually.

Uninstalling Applications

Over time, you may accumulate applications that you no longer need or want. Removing unused or unwanted applications can free up storage space and help declutter your system. Here's how to uninstall applications:

1. **Using Settings**:

   – Click on the "Start" button, then go to "Settings."
   – Select "Apps" in the "Settings" window.

2. **Select the Application to Uninstall**:

   – Scroll through the list of installed apps and select the application you want to uninstall.

3. **Uninstall**:

   – Click the "Uninstall" button associated with the selected application.
   – Confirm the uninstallation when prompted.

4. **Using the Control Panel**:

   – You can also uninstall applications through the Control Panel.
   – Type "Control Panel" in the search bar and open it.
   – Go to "Programs" > "Programs and Features."
   – Select the application you want to uninstall and click "Uninstall."

Removing Pre-installed or Built-in Apps

Some Windows 11 computers come with pre-installed or built-in applications that you may not need. While you can't uninstall all of them, you can remove some using PowerShell. Here's how:

1. **Open PowerShell as Administrator**:

   – Type "PowerShell" in the search bar.
   – Right-click on "Windows PowerShell" in the search results and select "Run as administrator."

2. **Check Installed Apps**:

   – Run the following command to list installed apps:

   ```
   Get-AppxPackage -AllUsers | Select-Object Name, PackageFullName
   ```

3. **Remove the App**:

   – To remove an app, use the following command (replace "PackageFullName" with the actual name of the app you want to uninstall):

   ```
   Remove-AppxPackage -Package PackageFullName
   ```

Cleaning Up Leftover Files

After uninstalling applications, it's a good practice to clean up any leftover files and folders to free up disk space. You can use Windows' built-in Disk Cleanup tool or third-party software for this purpose.

In conclusion, effectively managing installed applications in Windows 11 involves keeping them up to date for optimal performance and removing unnecessary ones to maintain a clean and organized system. Regularly reviewing and maintaining your application list helps ensure that your computer remains efficient and clutter-free.

4.4. Setting Default Applications and File Associations

In Windows 11, you can set default applications and file associations to control which app opens when you perform specific tasks or open certain file types. This allows you to customize your workflow and ensure that the right applications handle various tasks. In this section, we'll explore how to set default applications and manage file associations.

Setting Default Applications

To set a default application for a specific task or file type, follow these steps:

1. **Open Settings**:

    – Click on the "Start" button, then go to "Settings."

2. **Go to Apps**:

    – In the "Settings" window, select "Apps."

3. **Default Apps**:

    – In the left sidebar, click on "Default apps."

4. **Choose Default Apps**:

    – Under "Choose default apps," you can set default applications for various tasks, such as web browsing, email, maps, and music player.

5. **Select an App**:

    – Click on the current default app for a specific task or file type.
    – A list of available applications will appear. Choose the one you want to set as the default.

6. **Confirmation**:

    – Once you've selected the new default app, it will be set as the default for that task or file type.

Managing File Associations

Windows 11 allows you to control how different file types are associated with specific applications. This means you can choose which application opens when you double-click a file with a particular extension. Here's how to manage file associations:

1. **Open Settings**:

- Click on the "Start" button, then go to "Settings."
2. **Go to Apps**:
    - In the "Settings" window, select "Apps."
3. **Default Apps**:
    - In the left sidebar, click on "Default apps."
4. **Choose Default Apps by File Type**:
    - Scroll down and click on "Choose default apps by file type."
5. **Select a File Type**:
    - Scroll through the list of file types to find the one you want to change the association for.
6. **Choose an App**:
    - Click on the current default app for that file type.
    - Select the application you want to use to open files with that extension.
7. **Confirmation**:
    - The new app will now be associated with that file type.

Resetting Default Apps

If you want to reset default apps to their original settings, you can do so by following these steps:

1. **Open Settings**:
    - Click on the "Start" button, then go to "Settings."
2. **Go to Apps**:
    - In the "Settings" window, select "Apps."
3. **Default Apps**:
    - In the left sidebar, click on "Default apps."
4. **Reset**:
    - Scroll down to find the "Reset" button under "Reset to the Microsoft recommended defaults."
    - Click "Reset" to reset all default app associations to the recommended settings.

Customizing File Associations

If you want more control over file associations and default apps, you can customize them further:

1. **Right-Click a File**:

- Right-click on a file of the type you want to change the association for.

2. **Open With**:

    - From the context menu, select "Open with" and then "Choose another app."

3. **Choose an App**:

    - A dialog box will appear with a list of available applications. Select the one you want to use.

4. **Check "Always Use This App"**:

    - If you want this app to always open this type of file, check the box that says "Always use this app to open .[file extension] files."

5. **Open**:

    - Click "OK" to confirm your choice. The selected app will now open that file type by default.

By customizing default applications and file associations, you can tailor your Windows 11 experience to your preferences and work more efficiently with your preferred apps for specific tasks and file types.

4.5. Troubleshooting Common Application Issues

While using applications on Windows 11, you may encounter various issues that can disrupt your workflow. These issues can range from application crashes to performance problems. In this section, we'll explore common application-related problems and how to troubleshoot them effectively.

Application Crashes

Application crashes can occur for various reasons, such as software bugs, compatibility issues, or system resource limitations. Here's how to troubleshoot application crashes:

1. **Update the Application**: Ensure that the application is up to date. Developers often release updates to fix bugs and improve stability.

2. **Check Compatibility**: Verify if the application is compatible with Windows 11. Some older applications may require compatibility settings to run correctly.

3. **Check System Requirements**: Ensure that your computer meets the system requirements for the application. Lack of sufficient resources like RAM or CPU power can lead to crashes.

4. **Run as Administrator**: Right-click on the application's shortcut and select "Run as administrator." This can sometimes resolve permission-related issues.

5. **Check for Error Messages**: If the application displays an error message when crashing, take note of it. The error message can provide clues about the underlying issue.

6. **Clean Reinstall**: Uninstall the application, delete any remaining files and folders associated with it, and then reinstall it.

7. **Check for Conflicting Software**: Some software conflicts can lead to crashes. Disable or uninstall other recently installed software to check for conflicts.

Application Freezes or Slow Performance

If an application freezes or exhibits slow performance, you can try the following troubleshooting steps:

1. **Close Unnecessary Background Apps**: Close any other applications running in the background to free up system resources.

2. **Check for Updates**: Ensure that both the operating system and the application are updated to their latest versions.

3. **Restart the Application**: Close and reopen the application. This can sometimes resolve temporary performance issues.

4. **Restart Your Computer**: A full system restart can clear memory and resolve performance problems.

5. **Increase System Resources**: If an application regularly consumes a significant amount of system resources, consider upgrading your computer's hardware, such as adding more RAM or using a faster CPU.

6. **Scan for Malware**: Run a malware scan on your computer to ensure that malware is not affecting application performance.

7. **Check for Storage Space**: Ensure that you have enough free disk space on your system drive. Running low on storage can impact application performance.

Application Not Responding

When an application becomes unresponsive, you can take the following steps to address the issue:

1. **Wait for a Response**: Sometimes, an application may become unresponsive temporarily. Wait for a minute or two to see if it recovers.

2. **Force Close**: If the application remains unresponsive, you can force it to close by right-clicking its icon in the taskbar and selecting "Close window."

3. **Task Manager**: If the application doesn't respond to the above method, open the Task Manager by pressing Ctrl + Shift + Esc or Ctrl + Alt + Delete and

selecting "Task Manager." Find the application in the list, select it, and click "End Task."

4. **Restart the Application**: After forcefully closing the application, try restarting it to see if it functions correctly.

5. **Check for Updates**: Outdated applications may have known bugs that cause unresponsiveness. Check for and install any available updates.

6. **Disable Add-ons or Extensions**: If the application supports add-ons or extensions (e.g., web browsers), try disabling them to see if they are causing the problem.

7. **Reinstall the Application**: As a last resort, you can uninstall and then reinstall the application to ensure a clean installation.

Missing or Corrupted Files

If an application reports missing or corrupted files, you can address the issue as follows:

1. **Verify File Integrity**: Some applications include tools to verify the integrity of their files. Use these tools to check for and repair any corrupted files.

2. **Reinstall the Application**: If file corruption persists, uninstall the application and reinstall it from a trusted source.

3. **Check for System File Errors**: Run the "sfc /scannow" command in Command Prompt as an administrator to check and repair system file errors.

4. **Check for Disk Errors**: Run the "chkdsk /f" command in Command Prompt as an administrator to scan and repair disk errors.

By troubleshooting common application issues effectively, you can minimize disruptions to your workflow and ensure a smoother computing experience on Windows 11. It's essential to be patient and methodical when addressing these problems to identify and resolve the root causes.

Chapter 5: Mastering the Web with Microsoft Edge

5.1. Introduction to Microsoft Edge: Features and Capabilities

Microsoft Edge is the default web browser in Windows 11, and it offers a range of features and capabilities designed to enhance your web browsing experience. In this section, we'll introduce you to Microsoft Edge and explore its key features.

Microsoft Edge as the Default Browser

With Windows 11, Microsoft introduced Microsoft Edge as the default web browser, replacing Internet Explorer. This change brought significant improvements in terms of speed, security, and compatibility with modern web technologies.

Key Features of Microsoft Edge

Here are some of the key features and capabilities that Microsoft Edge offers:

1. *Speed and Performance:*
   - Microsoft Edge is built on the Chromium engine, which is known for its speed and efficiency. This means faster page loading times and smoother browsing.

2. *Integrated Search and Address Bar:*
   - Microsoft Edge combines the search bar and address bar into one, making it easy to search the web or enter website addresses.

3. *Customizable Start Page:*
   - You can personalize your start page with a customizable background, quick links to your favorite websites, and news feeds.

4. *Extensions:*
   - Microsoft Edge supports a wide range of extensions, allowing you to enhance its functionality with various add-ons and plugins.

5. *Collections:*
   - Collections allow you to organize and save web content, including links, text, and images, into a structured format for research or reference.

6. *Reading View:*
   - Reading View removes clutter from webpages, providing a clean and distraction-free reading experience.

7. *Web Capture:*
   - You can capture and annotate web content, including full webpages or specific sections, and save or share them.

8. Inking and Annotation:

- Microsoft Edge supports inking and annotation on webpages, allowing you to draw, highlight, and make notes directly on web content.

9. Vertical Tabs:

- Vertical Tabs provide a more organized way to manage and switch between open tabs.

10. Password Manager:

- Microsoft Edge includes a built-in password manager that can generate, store, and autofill passwords for your online accounts.

11. Privacy and Security:

- Microsoft Edge offers features like Tracking Prevention, SmartScreen, and HTTPS by default to enhance your online privacy and security.

12. Cortana Integration:

- Microsoft Edge integrates with Cortana, Microsoft's virtual assistant, to provide voice-activated browsing and personalized recommendations.

13. Compatibility Mode:

- Edge includes an Internet Explorer mode for legacy websites and applications that may not work correctly in modern browsers.

14. Developer Tools:

- For web developers, Microsoft Edge provides a robust set of developer tools for debugging and testing websites and web applications.

15. Cross-Device Syncing:

- You can sync your browsing history, bookmarks, and settings across devices, allowing you to continue your browsing session seamlessly.

16. Immersive Reader:

- Immersive Reader is a feature that improves the readability of webpages by focusing on the content and removing distractions.

In the following sections, we'll delve deeper into some of these features and provide tips on how to make the most of Microsoft Edge for your web browsing needs. Whether you're a casual internet user or a web developer, Microsoft Edge offers a range of tools and capabilities to enhance your online experience.

5.2. Optimizing Browser Settings for Performance and Security

To make the most of your web browsing experience with Microsoft Edge, it's essential to optimize your browser settings. This ensures that the browser runs smoothly, and your online activities remain secure. In this section, we'll explore various settings you can adjust in Microsoft Edge for both performance and security.

Performance Settings

1. Clear Browsing Data:

- Regularly clearing your browsing data, including cookies, cache, and history, can help keep your browser running smoothly. You can access this feature in Microsoft Edge by clicking on the three horizontal dots in the top-right corner, selecting "Settings," and then navigating to "Privacy, search, and services."

2. Hardware Acceleration:

- Hardware acceleration utilizes your computer's hardware resources, like the GPU, to render web content more efficiently. To enable or disable hardware acceleration in Microsoft Edge, go to "Settings" > "System."

3. Tab Management:

- Manage open tabs efficiently to prevent excessive memory usage. You can enable "Sleeping Tabs" in Microsoft Edge, which automatically puts background tabs to sleep to conserve resources.

4. Block Annoying Content:

- Use the built-in ad blocker in Microsoft Edge to block annoying ads and trackers that can slow down page loading. This can be found in "Settings" > "Privacy, search, and services."

Security Settings

1. Privacy Settings:

- Review and adjust your privacy settings to control how websites track your activity. In Microsoft Edge, go to "Settings" > "Privacy, search, and services" to configure privacy options like tracking prevention.

2. Secure Browsing:

- Ensure that you're using HTTPS by default whenever possible. Microsoft Edge automatically tries to use secure connections, but you can confirm this in "Settings" > "Privacy, search, and services" under the "Security" section.

3. Password Management:

- Use the built-in password manager in Microsoft Edge to generate and store strong, unique passwords for your online accounts. Enable synchronization to access your passwords across devices securely.

4. Security Updates:

- Keep Microsoft Edge up to date to ensure that you have the latest security patches and features. Microsoft Edge updates are typically delivered along with Windows updates.

5. SmartScreen Filter:

- Enable the SmartScreen Filter in Microsoft Edge to protect against phishing websites and malicious downloads. You can configure this in "Settings" > "Privacy, search, and services."

6. Browser Security Features:

- Explore additional browser security features like "Microsoft Defender SmartScreen" and "Windows Defender Antivirus Integration" to enhance your overall system security.

Customization and Preferences

1. Customize Your Start Page:

- Personalize your start page by selecting a custom background image, pinning favorite websites, and adding news topics of interest.

2. Manage Extensions:

- Carefully review and manage your browser extensions. Only install extensions from trusted sources, and regularly audit them for any suspicious behavior.

3. Search Engine:

- Choose your preferred search engine in Microsoft Edge's settings. You can select from popular search engines like Google, Bing, or others.

4. Sync Settings:

- If you use Microsoft Edge on multiple devices, consider enabling sync to have your bookmarks, history, passwords, and other settings synchronized across devices securely.

5. Accessibility:

- Customize browser settings for accessibility, such as text size, font style, and screen reading support, to ensure a comfortable browsing experience for all users.

By optimizing your Microsoft Edge settings for both performance and security, you can enjoy a faster and more secure web browsing experience. These adjustments allow you to tailor your browser to your preferences while safeguarding your online privacy and protecting your computer from potential threats.

5.3. Managing Bookmarks, History, and Extensions

Efficiently managing bookmarks, browsing history, and extensions is crucial to maintaining an organized and productive web browsing experience in Microsoft Edge. In this section, we'll explore how to manage these aspects of your browser effectively.

Managing Bookmarks

Adding Bookmarks:

- To bookmark a page in Microsoft Edge, click on the star icon in the address bar. You can choose a folder to save the bookmark or create a new one. Bookmarks help you quickly access your favorite websites.

Editing and Organizing Bookmarks:

- You can access your bookmarks by clicking the three horizontal lines in the top-right corner (the "Menu" button) and selecting "Favorites." From there, you can organize your bookmarks into folders, rename them, or delete them as needed.

Importing and Exporting Bookmarks:

- If you're switching from another browser or want to back up your bookmarks, you can import or export them in Microsoft Edge. Go to "Settings" > "Profiles" > "Import browser data" to access this feature.

Managing Browsing History

Viewing Browsing History:

- To view your browsing history, click on the three horizontal lines (the "Menu" button) and select "History." You can see a list of websites you've visited.

Clearing Browsing History:

- To clear your browsing history, go to "Settings" > "Privacy, search, and services" > "Clear browsing data." Here, you can select what to delete, such as history, cookies, and cached data.

Managing Individual History Entries:

- You can remove specific items from your history by right-clicking them and selecting "Delete." This is useful when you want to remove certain entries without clearing your entire history.

Managing Extensions

Installing Extensions:

- Microsoft Edge supports a wide range of extensions to enhance your browsing experience. To install extensions, click on the three horizontal lines (the "Menu" button) and select "Extensions." From there, you can explore and install extensions from the Microsoft Edge Add-ons Store.

Managing Extensions:

- In the Extensions menu, you can enable, disable, or remove installed extensions. Make sure to keep your extensions up to date for compatibility and security reasons.

Extension Settings:

- Some extensions may have their settings that you can configure. Click on the puzzle piece icon (Extensions) in the top-right corner to access your installed extensions and their settings.

Syncing Data Across Devices

- If you use Microsoft Edge on multiple devices, you can enable sync to keep your bookmarks, browsing history, and extensions consistent across all your devices. Go to "Settings" > "Profiles" > "Sync" to set up synchronization.

Backup and Restore

- It's a good practice to regularly back up your bookmarks and extension settings. You can do this by exporting your bookmarks and making a note of your installed extensions. In case of data loss or if you switch to a new device, you can easily restore your settings and preferences.

By effectively managing bookmarks, browsing history, and extensions in Microsoft Edge, you can streamline your web browsing experience, keep your favorite sites at your fingertips, and customize your browser to suit your needs. These tools allow you to make the most of your online activities while maintaining control over your browser's organization and functionality.

5.4. Using Reading Mode, Collections, and Other Unique Features

Microsoft Edge offers several unique features that can enhance your web browsing experience beyond the standard capabilities of a web browser. In this section, we'll explore features like Reading Mode, Collections, and other unique tools available in Microsoft Edge.

Reading Mode

Enabling Reading Mode:

- Reading Mode in Microsoft Edge provides a distraction-free reading experience by removing unnecessary clutter from webpages. To activate it, look for the "Reading view" icon in the address bar when you visit a page with a lot of content. Clicking this icon will switch the page to Reading Mode.

Customizing Reading Mode:

- You can customize the appearance of Reading Mode to suit your preferences. Click on the "Aa" icon in the Reading Mode toolbar to adjust text size, font, and background color.

- Immersive Reader is an extension of Reading Mode that focuses on improving the readability of webpages. It provides features like text-to-speech, adjustable spacing, and the ability to highlight and define words.

Collections

Creating Collections:

- Collections in Microsoft Edge allow you to organize and save web content like links, text snippets, and images for research, projects, or planning. To create a collection, click the Collections icon (the folder icon) in the top-right corner of the browser.

Adding Content to Collections:

- You can add content to your collections by simply dragging and dropping text or images from webpages into your collection. This feature makes it easy to gather information from multiple sources.

Organizing Collections:

- Collections can be organized by adding sections and notes, making it a powerful tool for research and content curation. You can also export collections as Word or Excel files for further use.

Web Capture

Using Web Capture:

- Web Capture allows you to capture and annotate web content, whether it's a full webpage or a specific section. Click on the Web Capture icon in the toolbar to start capturing.

Annotating Content:

- After capturing content, you can annotate it with highlights, text notes, and drawings. This is useful for research, making notes, or collaborating with others.

Vertical Tabs

Enabling Vertical Tabs:

- Vertical Tabs provide a more organized way to manage and switch between open tabs. You can enable this feature by clicking the Vertical Tabs icon on the left side of the browser.

Benefits of Vertical Tabs:

- Vertical Tabs save space and make it easier to identify and switch between tabs when you have multiple tabs open. You can also easily manage tab groups.

Collections Sharing

Sharing Collections:

- You can share your collections with others by clicking the "Share" button within a collection. This generates a link that others can access, making it a great tool for collaboration and sharing research findings.

Accessibility Features

Built-In Accessibility:

- Microsoft Edge offers various accessibility features, including customizable text size, font style, and screen reading support. These features ensure a comfortable browsing experience for all users.

Developer Tools

Robust Developer Tools:

- For web developers, Microsoft Edge provides a set of developer tools for debugging and testing websites and web applications. You can access these tools by pressing F12 or right-clicking and selecting "Inspect."

These unique features in Microsoft Edge go beyond basic web browsing, providing tools and capabilities that cater to various needs, from enhancing readability and research to supporting web development efforts. By exploring and utilizing these features, you can make your web browsing experience more efficient, productive, and tailored to your specific requirements.

5.5. Privacy and Security in Microsoft Edge

Privacy and security are essential aspects of web browsing, and Microsoft Edge offers several features and settings to help protect your online activities. In this section, we'll explore the privacy and security measures you can take while using Microsoft Edge.

Tracking Prevention

What is Tracking Prevention:

- Microsoft Edge includes a Tracking Prevention feature that helps protect your privacy by blocking third-party trackers and potentially harmful content from loading on webpages. This reduces the chances of websites tracking your online behavior.

Configuring Tracking Prevention:

- You can customize the level of tracking prevention in Microsoft Edge to suit your preferences. Go to "Settings" > "Privacy, search, and services" > "Tracking prevention" to adjust the settings.

Enhanced Privacy Settings

Privacy Settings Overview:

- Microsoft Edge offers a range of privacy settings that you can control to enhance your online privacy. These settings include options for managing cookies, site permissions, and more.

Clearing Browsing Data:

- Regularly clearing your browsing data, such as cookies and cached files, can help maintain your privacy. You can access the "Clear browsing data" feature in "Settings" > "Privacy, search, and services."

HTTPS by Default

What is HTTPS:

- Microsoft Edge prioritizes secure connections by default. It attempts to use HTTPS (Hypertext Transfer Protocol Secure) whenever possible. HTTPS encrypts your data, making it more difficult for third parties to intercept or manipulate.

Viewing Website Certificates:

- You can verify the security of a website by clicking on the padlock icon in the address bar. This allows you to view the website's security certificate details.

Password Manager

Using the Built-In Password Manager:

- Microsoft Edge includes a password manager that can generate, store, and autofill strong, unique passwords for your online accounts. This helps protect your accounts from unauthorized access.

Syncing Passwords Securely:

- If you use Microsoft Edge on multiple devices, you can sync your passwords securely across devices. This feature ensures that your passwords are readily available while maintaining their security.

SmartScreen Filter

Protecting Against Malicious Content:

- The SmartScreen Filter in Microsoft Edge helps protect you from phishing websites and malicious downloads by checking the safety of websites and files you encounter online.

- SmartScreen relies on a database of known threats and suspicious websites to warn you when you navigate to potentially harmful sites or download files.

Windows Defender Integration

Enhanced Security:

- Microsoft Edge integrates with Windows Defender, Microsoft's built-in antivirus and antimalware solution. This integration provides an additional layer of security when browsing the web.

Security Updates

Keeping Microsoft Edge Updated:

- Regularly updating Microsoft Edge ensures that you have the latest security patches and features. Microsoft Edge updates are typically delivered along with Windows updates.

By taking advantage of these privacy and security features in Microsoft Edge, you can browse the web with confidence, knowing that your online activities are protected. These measures help safeguard your personal information, enhance your privacy, and minimize the risks associated with online threats and malicious content.

Chapter 6: Productivity and Office Integration 6.1. Introduction to Microsoft Office Applications in Windows 11 6.2. Optimizing Your Workflow with Windows 11 and Office Tools 6.3. Using Outlook for Email and Calendar Management 6.4. Integrating OneNote for Note-Taking and Information Management 6.5. Collaborating with Teams and Shared Documents

---

Chapter 6: Productivity and Office Integration

6.1. Introduction to Microsoft Office Applications in Windows 11

Microsoft Office is a suite of productivity applications that includes popular tools like Word, Excel, PowerPoint, Outlook, and OneNote. In Windows 11, these applications are seamlessly integrated to enhance your productivity and make daily tasks more efficient. This section provides an overview of Microsoft Office applications in Windows 11, highlighting their key features and benefits.

Microsoft Word

Microsoft Word is a word processing application that allows you to create and edit documents with ease. Whether you're writing reports, letters, or essays, Word provides a wide range of formatting and styling options. Some key features of Word in Windows 11 include:

- **Rich Formatting:** Word offers extensive formatting options for text, images, and other elements in your documents. You can change fonts, colors, and styles to create visually appealing documents.

- **Collaboration:** With real-time collaboration features, you can work on documents simultaneously with others, making it easier to co-author and review content.

- **Templates:** Word provides numerous templates for various document types, saving you time and effort in creating professional-looking documents.

- **Integration:** Word seamlessly integrates with other Office applications, allowing you to embed Excel spreadsheets, PowerPoint presentations, and more directly into your documents.

Microsoft Excel

Microsoft Excel is a powerful spreadsheet application that enables you to analyze data, create charts, and perform complex calculations. Here are some key features of Excel in Windows 11:

- **Formulas and Functions:** Excel offers a vast library of built-in functions and the ability to create custom formulas to automate calculations.

- **Data Analysis:** You can use features like PivotTables and Power Query to analyze large datasets and gain valuable insights.

- **Data Visualization:** Excel allows you to create visually appealing charts and graphs to represent data effectively.

- **Integration:** Excel integrates seamlessly with other Office applications, making it easy to import data from Word or PowerPoint.

Microsoft PowerPoint

Microsoft PowerPoint is a presentation application that lets you create compelling slideshows and presentations. Whether for business meetings, lectures, or conferences, PowerPoint offers the following features in Windows 11:

- **Design Templates:** PowerPoint provides a wide range of templates and themes to create visually striking presentations.

- **Transitions and Animations:** You can add transitions and animations to your slides to make your presentations engaging and dynamic.

- **Presenter View:** When delivering presentations, the Presenter View allows you to see speaker notes, upcoming slides, and a timer, making it easier to deliver your message effectively.

- **Collaboration:** PowerPoint supports real-time collaboration, allowing multiple users to work on a presentation simultaneously.

Microsoft Outlook

Microsoft Outlook is an email and calendar application that helps you manage your emails, appointments, and tasks. In Windows 11, Outlook offers the following features:

- **Email Management:** Outlook provides tools for organizing, filtering, and categorizing emails, making it easier to stay on top of your inbox.

- **Calendar Integration:** You can schedule appointments, meetings, and events in Outlook and sync them with your Windows 11 calendar.

- **Task Management:** Outlook's task feature allows you to create to-do lists and set reminders to stay organized.

- **Integration:** Outlook seamlessly integrates with other Office applications, enabling you to send documents, schedule meetings, and more directly from your email.

Microsoft OneNote

Microsoft OneNote is a digital note-taking application that allows you to capture ideas, create to-do lists, and organize your thoughts. In Windows 11, OneNote offers the following features:

- **Note Organization:** OneNote provides notebooks, sections, and pages to structure your notes and keep them organized.

- **Ink Support:** If you have a touchscreen device, you can use a stylus or your finger to draw and write directly in OneNote.

- **Syncing Across Devices:** Your OneNote notes sync across all your devices, ensuring you can access your information wherever you are.

- **Collaboration:** OneNote supports collaborative note-taking, making it easy to share and work on notes with others.

Microsoft Office applications in Windows 11 are essential tools for productivity, whether you're a student, professional, or enthusiast. Understanding their capabilities and integration with the Windows 11 environment can help you streamline your work and achieve your goals more efficiently.

6.2. Optimizing Your Workflow with Windows 11 and Office Tools

Windows 11 is designed to enhance your productivity by seamlessly integrating with Microsoft Office applications, including Word, Excel, PowerPoint, Outlook, and OneNote. In this section, we'll explore how you can optimize your workflow using these tools within the Windows 11 environment.

Unified Experience

One of the key advantages of using Microsoft Office applications in Windows 11 is the unified experience they offer. You can easily switch between applications and access your documents, emails, and notes with a consistent user interface. This unified experience ensures that you can work efficiently without the need for constant context switching.

Quick Access to Recent Documents

Windows 11's Start Menu and Taskbar provide quick access to your recently opened documents, making it convenient to resume your work. Whether it's a Word document, Excel spreadsheet, or PowerPoint presentation, you can pin frequently used files for even faster access.

Cortana Integration

Windows 11's built-in virtual assistant, Cortana, can help you perform tasks more efficiently. You can use voice commands to open Office applications, create new documents, send emails, or schedule appointments in Outlook. Cortana's integration with Office tools adds a new dimension to hands-free productivity.

Multi-Monitor Support

If you work with multiple monitors, Windows 11's improved multi-monitor support complements your productivity. You can extend your Office applications across screens, allowing you to view your documents, emails, and spreadsheets simultaneously, boosting your multitasking capabilities.

Snap Layouts and Snap Groups

Windows 11 introduces Snap Layouts and Snap Groups, features that enhance window management. You can organize your Office applications and documents side by side using Snap Layouts. Snap Groups allow you to group related Office apps and quickly switch between tasks, improving your workflow efficiency.

Virtual Desktops

Virtual desktops in Windows 11 enable you to create separate workspaces for different projects or tasks. You can dedicate one virtual desktop to your Office applications, making it easier to stay organized and focused on your work. Switching between virtual desktops is seamless, enhancing your productivity.

Enhanced Collaboration

Microsoft Office applications in Windows 11 offer enhanced collaboration features. Real-time co-authoring in Word, Excel, and PowerPoint allows multiple users to edit documents simultaneously, facilitating teamwork and speeding up project completion.

Customization and Integration

You can customize the Office applications to suit your preferences and workflow. Configure keyboard shortcuts, set default templates, and personalize the ribbon interface to streamline your tasks further. Integration with Microsoft Teams also enables seamless communication and collaboration with colleagues.

Cloud Integration

Office applications in Windows 11 seamlessly integrate with Microsoft's cloud services, such as OneDrive and SharePoint. This integration ensures that your documents are automatically synced and backed up in the cloud, making them accessible from any device with an internet connection.

Security and Compliance

Windows 11 and Microsoft Office offer robust security and compliance features. You can protect your sensitive documents with encryption and access controls, ensuring that your data remains secure. Additionally, compliance features help you meet regulatory requirements in your industry.

In summary, Windows 11 and Microsoft Office applications provide a powerful ecosystem for optimizing your workflow and enhancing productivity. The seamless integration, unified experience, and numerous features make it easier than ever to create, collaborate, and manage your work efficiently within the Windows 11 environment. Whether you're a student, professional, or business user, these tools can help you achieve your goals with greater ease and efficiency.

6.3. Using Outlook for Email and Calendar Management

Microsoft Outlook is a powerful email and calendar application that is an integral part of Microsoft Office in Windows 11. In this section, we will explore how to effectively use Outlook for managing your email communication and calendar events.

Email Management

Outlook provides a comprehensive set of tools for managing your email efficiently:

1. **Unified Inbox**: Outlook consolidates all your email accounts into one unified inbox, making it convenient to view and manage multiple email addresses from a single location.

2. **Focused Inbox**: The Focused Inbox feature automatically categorizes your emails into two tabs: Focused (important emails) and Other (less important emails). This helps you prioritize your messages and focus on what matters most.

3. **Search and Filters**: Outlook offers powerful search capabilities, allowing you to quickly find emails using keywords, sender names, or other criteria. Filters and rules can help you automatically organize incoming emails into folders.

4. **Email Templates**: Create and save email templates for commonly used messages, such as meeting requests or responses to frequently asked questions, saving you time on repetitive tasks.

5. **Attachments and Cloud Integration**: Easily attach files to your emails, and Outlook integrates seamlessly with OneDrive, making it convenient to share large files as cloud links instead of attachments.

6. **Flags and Categories**: Use flags to mark important emails for follow-up and categories to categorize and color-code emails for better organization.

7. **Conversation View**: Group related emails into conversations, allowing you to see the entire email thread for better context.

Calendar Management

Outlook's calendar features help you stay organized and manage your schedule effectively:

1. **Event Scheduling**: Create and manage appointments, meetings, and events in your calendar. You can set reminders and specify locations and attendees.

2. **Sharing and Collaboration**: Share your calendar with colleagues or family members, and schedule meetings that automatically find the best time for all participants.

3. **Recurrence and Reminders**: Set recurring events, such as weekly team meetings or monthly reminders, to automate the scheduling process.

4. **Busy and Free Times**: Check the availability of colleagues or resources to avoid scheduling conflicts.

5. **Color Coding**: Assign different colors to events or categories for visual differentiation and easy identification.

6. **Sync Across Devices**: Outlook's calendar syncs across all your devices, ensuring that you have access to your schedule wherever you go.

7. **Calendar Views**: Choose from various calendar views, such as day, week, month, or agenda view, to see your schedule in the most convenient format.

Integration with Office Suite

Outlook seamlessly integrates with other Microsoft Office applications, allowing you to:

1. **Attach Files**: Easily attach documents from your OneDrive or SharePoint to calendar events or emails, ensuring that you always have access to the latest files.

2. **Meeting Scheduling**: Schedule and manage meetings directly from your email or calendar, including the ability to send meeting invitations and track responses.

3. **Email and Calendar Integration**: Outlook allows you to convert emails into calendar events or tasks, helping you turn important messages into actionable items.

4. **Task Management**: Use Outlook's task feature to create to-do lists, set due dates, and prioritize tasks. Tasks also integrate with your calendar for better time management.

5. **Contact Management**: Keep track of your contacts and easily access their information when composing emails or scheduling meetings.

In conclusion, Microsoft Outlook is a versatile and feature-rich application for email and calendar management in Windows 11. Whether you're managing your work schedule, coordinating with colleagues, or staying on top of your personal appointments, Outlook offers the tools and functionality you need to streamline your communication and time management tasks.

6.4. Integrating OneNote for Note-Taking and Information Management

Microsoft OneNote is a versatile digital note-taking application that seamlessly integrates with Windows 11 and offers a range of features for capturing, organizing, and sharing your notes and information. In this section, we will explore how to effectively integrate OneNote into your Windows 11 workflow for enhanced note-taking and information management.

Overview of OneNote

OneNote is a digital notebook that allows you to create and organize notes, drawings, clippings, and more. Here's an overview of its key features:

1. **Notebook Structure**: OneNote uses a notebook-based structure, where you can create multiple notebooks, each containing sections and pages. This hierarchical organization makes it easy to categorize and locate your notes.

2. **Text and Media**: Create text-based notes, add images, embed videos, and record audio directly within your notes. This multimedia support enhances your ability to capture information.

3. **Ink Support**: If you have a touch-enabled device or a stylus, OneNote offers robust ink support, allowing you to write or draw on your notes naturally.

4. **Tagging and Searching**: Use tags to categorize and mark important content within your notes. OneNote's powerful search feature helps you quickly find specific notes or tagged items.

5. **Sync Across Devices**: Your OneNote notebooks sync across all your Windows devices, ensuring that your notes are accessible wherever you go.

6. **Collaboration**: Share notebooks with others and collaborate on notes in real-time, making it an ideal tool for team projects or group study sessions.

Integrating OneNote with Windows 11

To make the most of OneNote within Windows 11, follow these integration tips:

1. **Quick Access**: Pin OneNote to your Windows taskbar or Start menu for quick access. This allows you to open OneNote with a single click and start taking notes instantly.

2. **Note Clipping**: Use the OneNote Web Clipper extension in Microsoft Edge to capture web content, such as articles, images, and web pages, directly into your OneNote notebooks for reference or research.

3. **Integration with Office Suite**: OneNote seamlessly integrates with other Office applications. You can insert Excel spreadsheets, Word documents, PowerPoint presentations, and Outlook emails into your notes, creating a comprehensive knowledge repository.

4. **OneNote Printer**: Install the "Send to OneNote" printer driver, which allows you to print documents, web pages, or any content from other applications directly into your OneNote notebooks as printable pages.

5. **Digital Inking**: If you have a touchscreen device or stylus, leverage OneNote's digital inking capabilities for sketching diagrams, annotating documents, or taking handwritten notes.

6. **Voice Notes**: Use OneNote's audio recording feature to capture lectures, meetings, or personal voice notes, and sync them across your devices for easy access.

7. **Integration with Cortana**: You can use Cortana, the virtual assistant in Windows 11, to create reminders and tasks in OneNote, making it easier to manage your to-do lists.

Organizing and Managing Information

OneNote offers several features to help you organize and manage your notes effectively:

1. **Notebook Sections**: Create separate sections within your notebooks for different topics, projects, or subjects.

2. **Page Templates**: OneNote provides various pre-designed templates, such as meeting notes, to-do lists, and project plans, to streamline note-taking and organization.

3. **Table of Contents**: Generate a table of contents within a section to quickly navigate through your notes and find specific information.

4. **Tagging System**: Utilize OneNote's tagging system to mark action items, deadlines, or important content. You can create custom tags to suit your needs.

5. **Notebook Backup**: Regularly back up your OneNote notebooks to ensure that your data is safe. You can use OneDrive for cloud backup and recovery.

6. **Password Protection**: Protect sensitive notes by adding password protection to specific sections or entire notebooks.

In conclusion, integrating Microsoft OneNote into your Windows 11 workflow enhances your note-taking and information management capabilities. Whether you're a student, professional, or anyone who needs to capture and organize information, OneNote's versatile features and seamless integration with Windows 11 make it a valuable tool for productivity and knowledge management.

6.5. Collaborating with Teams and Shared Documents

Collaboration is a crucial aspect of modern work, and Windows 11 provides seamless integration with Microsoft Teams, a powerful collaboration platform. In this section, we'll explore how Windows 11 users can leverage Microsoft Teams for efficient teamwork and document sharing.

What is Microsoft Teams?

Microsoft Teams is a unified communication and collaboration platform that brings together chat, video conferencing, file sharing, and app integration into a single workspace. It is an integral part of Microsoft 365 and offers features that enable teams to work together effectively, whether in the office or remotely.

Getting Started with Microsoft Teams

1. *Installation*: *Microsoft Teams can be installed on Windows 11 as a standalone desktop application or accessed through a web browser. To install the desktop app, you can download it from the official Microsoft Teams website.*

2. *Signing In*: *You will need a Microsoft 365 account to sign in to Teams. Once signed in, you can create or join teams, channels, and start collaborating.*

Features of Microsoft Teams

1. *Chat and Messaging*: *Teams provides real-time chat and messaging, allowing team members to communicate one-on-one or in groups. You can share messages, images, files, and even schedule meetings directly in chat.*

2. *Video Conferencing*: *Teams offers video conferencing capabilities, making it easy to conduct virtual meetings, webinars, and presentations. You can schedule meetings in advance or start an impromptu meeting.*

3. *Team Channels*: *Teams are organized into channels, which are dedicated spaces for specific projects, departments, or topics. Each channel can have its own set of conversations and files.*

4. *File Sharing and Collaboration*: *Teams seamlessly integrates with OneDrive and SharePoint, allowing team members to share and collaborate on documents, spreadsheets, and presentations in real time.*

5. *App Integration*: *You can extend Teams' functionality by integrating various apps and services, such as Trello, Asana, and more, directly into your workspace.*

6. *Customization*: *Customize your Teams experience by adding tabs, connectors, and bots to enhance productivity and streamline workflows.*

Collaborative Document Editing

One of the standout features of Microsoft Teams is its collaborative document editing capabilities. Here's how you can collaborate on documents within Teams:

1. **Uploading Files**: You can upload files to a Teams channel or chat. These files can be Word documents, Excel spreadsheets, PowerPoint presentations, and more.

2. **Real-Time Editing**: Once a document is uploaded, team members can open it within Teams and edit it simultaneously. Changes made by one person are instantly visible to others in real time.

3. **Commenting and Chat**: Users can leave comments within the document or use the chat feature to discuss changes, ask questions, or provide feedback while working on the document.

4. **Version History**: Teams automatically tracks changes and maintains a version history of the document. You can access previous versions and restore them if needed.

5. **Integration with Office Apps**: Teams integrates seamlessly with the Office suite, so you can open documents in Word, Excel, or PowerPoint directly from Teams for more advanced editing.

6. **Co-Authoring**: Co-authoring is supported across Word, Excel, and PowerPoint, allowing multiple team members to work on the same document simultaneously.

Benefits of Collaborating with Teams

- **Efficient Communication**: Teams centralizes communication, reducing the need for scattered emails and messages.

- **Enhanced Productivity**: Real-time collaboration on documents and integration with Office apps streamline work processes.

- **Secure Environment**: Teams provides robust security features to protect sensitive information and documents.

- **Remote Work**: Teams is well-suited for remote work, enabling teams to collaborate effectively from anywhere.

In conclusion, Microsoft Teams is a valuable tool for collaborative work and document sharing in Windows 11. Its integration with Office apps, real-time editing, and communication features make it an essential platform for modern teams, whether they are working in the same office or remotely. Teams helps enhance productivity and streamline teamwork by providing a unified workspace for communication and collaboration.

Chapter 7: Multimedia and Entertainment

7.1. Using Windows Media Player and Groove Music

Windows 11 offers various multimedia and entertainment features to enhance your media playback experience. In this section, we'll explore two key applications: Windows Media Player and Groove Music. These applications allow you to manage and enjoy your music and video collections on your Windows 11 device.

Windows Media Player

Overview:

Windows Media Player (WMP) is a versatile media player application that comes pre-installed with Windows 11. It supports a wide range of audio and video file formats, making it a go-to choice for many users to play their media content.

Using Windows Media Player:

1. **Opening Windows Media Player**: To launch Windows Media Player, simply type "Windows Media Player" into the Start Menu search bar and click on the app when it appears.

2. **Media Library**: Windows Media Player maintains a media library where you can organize your music and video files. You can add files to the library by clicking on the "Organize" menu and selecting "Manage libraries."

3. **Playing Media**: To play media files, click on the "Music" or "Video" tab in the player's interface and browse your library to select the file you want to play. Alternatively, you can drag and drop files into the player.

4. **Playback Controls**: Use the playback controls at the bottom of the player to pause, play, skip forward or backward, adjust volume, and toggle full-screen mode.

5. **Creating Playlists**: Windows Media Player allows you to create playlists to organize your favorite songs. You can add songs to playlists by right-clicking on a song and selecting "Add to" > "Playlist."

6. **Burning CDs**: WMP also provides the option to create audio CDs by burning your selected songs to a blank CD. This is useful for creating personalized music CDs.

7. **Syncing Devices**: You can use Windows Media Player to sync music and videos with portable devices like MP3 players, smartphones, and USB drives.

8. **Media Information**: WMP automatically retrieves media information and album art from the internet for your music files, providing a rich media experience.

Groove Music

Groove Music is a music streaming application developed by Microsoft. It offers a vast catalog of songs that you can stream, as well as the ability to purchase and download music. While it's not pre-installed on Windows 11, you can download it from the Microsoft Store.

Using Groove Music:

1. **Installation**: To install Groove Music, open the Microsoft Store, search for "Groove Music," and click "Install."

2. **Streaming Music**: Once installed, you can use Groove Music to stream music from a wide range of genres and artists. You can explore playlists, create your own, and discover new music.

3. **Music Purchases**: Groove Music allows you to purchase and download songs and albums directly from the app. Your purchased music is stored in your library.

4. **Offline Listening**: You can download music for offline listening, which is handy for situations where you don't have an internet connection.

5. **Groove Pass**: Groove Music Pass, a subscription service, offers ad-free streaming and unlimited downloads. It's a great option for avid music listeners.

6. **Radio Stations**: Groove Music offers curated radio stations based on your music preferences, helping you discover new songs and artists.

Which One to Use?

The choice between Windows Media Player and Groove Music depends on your preferences and needs:

- Use **Windows Media Player** if you have a collection of media files stored on your computer and want a simple player to manage and play them.

- Use **Groove Music** if you prefer streaming music, discovering new tracks, or purchasing and downloading songs. Groove Music offers a more extensive music catalog and additional features for music enthusiasts.

In conclusion, Windows 11 provides multimedia and entertainment options through Windows Media Player and Groove Music. Whether you want to manage your existing media library or explore a vast world of music, these applications cater to different preferences, ensuring you have a satisfying multimedia experience on your Windows 11 device.

7.2. Photo and Video Editing with Windows 11 Tools

Windows 11 comes with built-in tools for photo and video editing, making it convenient for users to enhance and customize their media content without the need for third-party software. In this section, we'll explore the photo and video editing capabilities that Windows 11 offers.

Photo Editing with Photos App

Overview:

The Photos app in Windows 11 allows you to edit and enhance your photos effortlessly. It offers a variety of tools and features to adjust, crop, apply filters, and make your photos look their best.

Editing Photos:

1. **Opening Photos**: To open the Photos app, simply type "Photos" into the Start Menu search bar and click on the app when it appears.

2. **Selecting a Photo**: Navigate to the photo you want to edit and open it within the Photos app.

3. **Editing Tools**: Click on the "Edit & Create" button at the top-right corner to access editing tools. Here are some key features:

   – **Crop & Rotate**: Crop your photo to remove unwanted areas or straighten it. You can also rotate the image.

   – **Filters**: Apply various filters to change the mood and style of your photo.

   – **Adjust**: Fine-tune aspects like brightness, contrast, saturation, and color balance.

   – **Effects**: Add creative effects like vignettes, spotlights, and more.

   – **Text and Draw**: Overlay text or drawings on your photo.

   – **Enhance**: Let the app automatically enhance your photo with one click.

   – **Spot Fix**: Remove blemishes or unwanted objects with the spot fix tool.

4. **Saving Edits**: Once you're satisfied with your edits, click the "Save a Copy" button to keep the original photo intact. You can also choose to overwrite the original if needed.

Video Editing with Video Editor App

Overview:

Windows 11 includes a Video Editor app that allows you to edit your videos with ease. You can trim, add text, insert transitions, and apply effects to create engaging videos.

Editing Videos:

1. **Opening Video Editor**: To open the Video Editor app, search for "Video Editor" in the Start Menu and launch the app.

2. **Importing Videos**: Click on the "+ New Video Project" button and give your project a name. Then, import the video clips you want to edit.

3. **Editing Tools**: Here are some of the editing tools available in Video Editor:

    – **Trimming**: Drag the video clips to the timeline, and you can trim them by selecting the clip and using the trim handles.

    – **Adding Text**: You can add text overlays to your video for titles, captions, or descriptions.

    – **Transitions**: Apply smooth transitions between video clips for a professional look.

    – **Filters**: Enhance your video with various filters and effects.

    – **Motion**: Add motion to your photos within the video for a dynamic feel.

    – **Music**: Import music tracks to accompany your video.

    – **Voiceover**: Record a voiceover to narrate your video.

4. **Preview and Export**: After making your edits, preview your video and make any necessary adjustments. Once satisfied, click the "Export" button to save your edited video.

Which One to Use?

The choice between using the Photos app and Video Editor app depends on your editing needs:

- Use the **Photos app** for quick and easy photo enhancements, adjustments, and creative effects.

- Use the **Video Editor app** when working with video content, as it provides a range of video-specific editing tools like trimming, transitions, and text overlays.

With these built-in editing tools, Windows 11 empowers users to enhance their photos and videos without the need for third-party software, making it a versatile platform for multimedia content creation and customization.

7.3. Streaming Media: Movies, TV Shows, and Music

Windows 11 provides various options for streaming movies, TV shows, and music, allowing users to access their favorite entertainment content seamlessly. In this section, we'll explore the built-in streaming capabilities and popular streaming services available on Windows 11.

Streaming Media Services

Built-In Media Apps:

Windows 11 includes pre-installed media apps that enable users to stream content from various sources:

1. **Movies & TV**: The "Movies & TV" app allows users to rent or purchase movies and TV shows from the Microsoft Store. It also supports playback of personal video files.

2. **Microsoft Store**: Users can browse and purchase movies, TV shows, and music directly from the Microsoft Store. Once purchased, these digital media files can be accessed on Windows 11 devices.

Popular Streaming Services:

In addition to built-in apps, users can access popular streaming services through dedicated apps or web browsers on Windows 11:

1. **Netflix**: Netflix offers a dedicated app for Windows 11, providing access to a vast library of movies, TV series, and documentaries. Users can stream content in high-quality video.

2. **Amazon Prime Video**: Amazon Prime Video also offers a dedicated app for Windows 11, allowing users to stream movies, TV shows, and Amazon Originals.

3. **Disney+**: Disney+ subscribers can enjoy their favorite Disney, Pixar, Marvel, and Star Wars content through the Disney+ app on Windows 11.

4. **Spotify**: Music enthusiasts can stream their favorite songs and playlists using the Spotify app on Windows 11. It offers both free and premium subscription options.

5. **YouTube**: YouTube can be accessed through web browsers on Windows 11, offering a wide range of user-generated and professional content.

Using Built-In Media Apps

Movies & TV App:

1. Open the "Movies & TV" app.
2. Browse or search for the movie or TV show you want to watch.
3. Click on the title to view details and options.
4. Choose to rent, purchase, or play if you already own the content.

5. Follow on-screen instructions to complete the transaction or start watching.

Microsoft Store:
1. Open the Microsoft Store.
2. Browse or search for movies, TV shows, or music albums.
3. Click on the desired title to view details and options.
4. Choose to purchase or rent (for movies and TV shows) or purchase (for music albums).
5. Follow the on-screen prompts to complete your purchase or rental.

Streaming from Dedicated Apps
1. Open the dedicated streaming app (e.g., Netflix, Amazon Prime Video).
2. Sign in to your account or create one if you're a new user.
3. Browse or search for the content you want to watch.
4. Select the title to start streaming.

Streaming through Web Browsers
1. Open a web browser (e.g., Microsoft Edge, Google Chrome).
2. Visit the website of your preferred streaming service (e.g., Netflix, YouTube).
3. Sign in to your account.
4. Browse and select the content you want to stream.

Windows 11 provides a versatile platform for accessing and streaming media content, ensuring that users can enjoy their favorite movies, TV shows, and music with ease. Whether using built-in apps or dedicated streaming services, the options are plentiful for entertainment enthusiasts.

7.4. Gaming on Windows 11: Xbox Integration and Game Pass

Gaming is an integral part of the Windows 11 experience, and the operating system offers robust features for both casual and hardcore gamers. In this section, we'll delve into gaming on Windows 11, with a focus on Xbox integration and the Xbox Game Pass service.

Xbox Integration

Windows 11 seamlessly integrates with Xbox, Microsoft's gaming ecosystem, providing a unified gaming experience across devices. Here's what you need to know about Xbox integration on Windows 11:

Xbox App:
- The **Xbox app** comes pre-installed on Windows 11 and serves as your gaming hub. It allows you to access your Xbox Live account, manage your gaming library, and connect with friends.

- You can use the Xbox app to **view and manage your Xbox Live profile**, including your friends list, achievements, and gaming activity.

- It provides a **social platform** for gamers, allowing you to chat with friends, create and join parties, and even stream your gameplay to others.

Xbox Game Bar:
- The **Xbox Game Bar** is an overlay that you can activate while playing games. It offers a range of features, including **capturing screenshots and videos**, **monitoring system performance**, and **interacting with friends**.

- Pressing **Win+G** activates the Xbox Game Bar during gameplay, providing quick access to its features.

Game Mode:
- **Game Mode** is a Windows 11 feature that optimizes your system's resources for gaming. It prioritizes CPU and GPU resources for your game, ensuring a smoother gaming experience.

- You can enable Game Mode for a specific game by **pressing Win+G** to open the Xbox Game Bar and selecting the Game Mode option.

Xbox Game Pass

Xbox Game Pass is a subscription service that grants you access to a vast library of games for a monthly fee. Here's what you need to know about Xbox Game Pass on Windows 11:

- Xbox Game Pass offers **two tiers**: **Xbox Game Pass for Console** and **Xbox Game Pass for PC**. The latter is specifically tailored for Windows 11 gamers.

- With Xbox Game Pass for PC, you gain access to a diverse collection of games, including Xbox Game Studios titles on the day of release.

- You can **download and play games** from the Xbox Game Pass library directly on your Windows 11 device, ensuring a high-quality gaming experience.

- The service is regularly updated with new titles, providing a continuous stream of fresh gaming content.

- Xbox Game Pass subscribers also enjoy **exclusive discounts** on game purchases and additional content.

Gaming Accessories

Windows 11 supports a wide range of gaming accessories, including controllers, keyboards, mice, and more. Here are some additional gaming features:

- **Controller Support**: Windows 11 has extensive controller support, including Xbox controllers and various third-party options.

- **DirectX 12 Ultimate**: Windows 11 incorporates DirectX 12 Ultimate, delivering enhanced graphics and performance for DirectX 12-compatible games.

- **Auto HDR**: Auto High Dynamic Range (HDR) support is available for compatible displays, enriching your gaming visuals.

- **FPS Boost**: Some games in the Xbox Game Pass library offer FPS Boost, increasing frame rates for smoother gameplay.

Windows 11 caters to gamers of all levels, from casual players enjoying the Xbox Game Pass library to hardcore gamers taking advantage of the system's advanced gaming features. With Xbox integration, Game Mode, and a diverse selection of gaming accessories, Windows 11 provides a dynamic gaming ecosystem.

7.5. Customizing Sound Settings and Audio Enhancements

Windows 11 offers a range of sound settings and audio enhancements that allow you to tailor your audio experience to your preferences. Whether you're using your computer for entertainment, communication, or work, understanding and customizing these settings can greatly enhance your overall experience. In this section, we will explore various sound settings and audio enhancements in Windows 11.

Sound Settings

1. *Volume Control:*
   - You can adjust the system volume by clicking on the **speaker icon** in the taskbar and dragging the slider.

2. *Sound Output Devices:*
   - Windows 11 allows you to choose the default sound output device. You can do this by right-clicking the speaker icon and selecting **Open Sound settings**. Under **Output**, you can choose your preferred audio output device.

3. *Sound Input Devices:*
   - Similarly, you can choose the default sound input device for recording audio. This is useful for microphones and other recording devices. You can manage this in the **Sound settings** under **Input**.

4. *Sound Mixer:*
   - You can control the volume of individual apps and system sounds using the **Sound Mixer**. Right-click the speaker icon and select **Open Volume Mixer** to access this feature.

5. Advanced Sound Settings:

- For more advanced sound settings, click on **Sound settings** and navigate to **Advanced sound options**. Here, you can customize app volumes and input/output preferences.

Spatial Sound

Windows 11 supports spatial sound, which can provide a more immersive audio experience, especially for games and multimedia content. To enable spatial sound:

1. Open **Sound settings**.
2. Under **Output**, click on the **Device properties** link next to your audio output device.
3. In the device properties, go to the **Spatial sound** tab and select the desired spatial sound format, such as Windows Sonic for Headphones or Dolby Atmos.

Audio Enhancements

1. Equalizer:

- Windows 11 includes a built-in **Equalizer** that allows you to fine-tune audio frequencies. To access it, right-click the speaker icon, select **Open Sound settings**, and then click on **Device properties** under **Output**. In the device properties, you can find the **Equalizer** option.

2. Enhancements:

- In the **Sound settings**, under **Advanced sound options**, you can access audio enhancements. These include options like **Bass Boost**, **Virtual Surround**, and **Loudness Equalization**. You can enable or disable these enhancements based on your preferences.

3. Communications Tab:

- Under **Sound settings**, in the **Communications** tab, you can configure how Windows handles audio during calls and communication activities. You can choose to reduce other sounds when making or receiving calls to ensure clarity.

Troubleshooting Audio Issues

If you encounter audio problems in Windows 11, there are built-in troubleshooting tools that can help you diagnose and resolve them. You can access these tools by right-clicking the speaker icon, selecting **Troubleshoot sound problems**, and following the on-screen instructions.

Customizing sound settings and using audio enhancements in Windows 11 can significantly improve your audio experience, whether you're gaming, watching movies, or working on projects that require clear communication. Take advantage of these features to tailor your audio to your liking and ensure a more enjoyable computing experience.

Chapter 8: Networking and Connectivity

8.1. Understanding Network Settings in Windows 11

Windows 11 provides a robust set of network settings and features to ensure that you can connect to various networks, share resources, and access the internet seamlessly. Understanding these network settings is essential, whether you're using a wired Ethernet connection, Wi-Fi, or managing network resources. In this section, we will explore the network settings in Windows 11.

Network and Internet Settings

To access network settings:

1. Click on the **Start** button and select **Settings** (the gear-shaped icon).
2. In the Settings window, select **Network & Internet**.

Here, you will find several categories of network settings and information about your current network connection.

1. Status:

- The **Status** category provides an overview of your current network connection. You can see if you're connected to the internet, the type of connection (Wi-Fi or Ethernet), and access troubleshooting tools.

2. Wi-Fi:

- Under **Wi-Fi**, you can manage your wireless network connections. You can view available Wi-Fi networks, connect to a network, and configure Wi-Fi settings.

3. Ethernet:

- If you're using a wired Ethernet connection, the **Ethernet** category allows you to manage Ethernet settings, including the ability to configure IP addresses and DNS settings.

4. VPN:

- Windows 11 includes built-in support for Virtual Private Networks (VPNs). Under **VPN**, you can add, configure, and connect to VPN connections for enhanced privacy and security.

5. Dial-up:

- If you're using a dial-up connection, this category allows you to configure and manage dial-up connections.

Network Troubleshooting

Windows 11 offers built-in network troubleshooting tools to help you diagnose and resolve network-related issues. If you encounter problems with your network connection, consider the following steps:

1. In the **Network & Internet** settings, scroll down to the **Advanced network settings** section.
2. Click on **Network troubleshooter** to launch the troubleshooting tool.
3. Follow the on-screen instructions to identify and resolve network problems.

Network Sharing and Discovery

Windows 11 allows you to share files, printers, and other resources on your local network. To enable network sharing and discovery:

1. In the **Network & Internet** settings, click on **Sharing options**.
2. You can configure network profile settings such as network discovery, file and printer sharing, and public folder sharing. Adjust these settings based on your network needs.

Network Adapters and Drivers

Managing network adapters and their drivers is crucial for ensuring a stable and reliable network connection. If you encounter network issues, consider the following:

1. In the **Network & Internet** settings, click on **Change adapter options** under **Advanced network settings**.
2. Here, you can view and manage your network adapters. If you suspect driver issues, update or reinstall the network adapter drivers.

Advanced Network Settings

For advanced users or specific network configurations, Windows 11 provides access to additional network settings:

1. In the **Network & Internet** settings, click on **Advanced network settings**.
2. Here, you can configure options such as proxy settings, IP address configuration, and network reset.

Understanding and effectively using these network settings in Windows 11 will empower you to manage your network connections, troubleshoot issues, and optimize your network experience, whether it's for personal use or in a business environment.

8.2. Setting Up and Managing Wi-Fi and Ethernet Connections

In Windows 11, managing Wi-Fi and Ethernet connections is an essential part of ensuring that your device is connected to the internet or local network. Whether you're setting up a new connection or troubleshooting an existing one, Windows 11 offers a user-friendly interface for managing network connections. In this section, we will explore how to set up and manage both Wi-Fi and Ethernet connections.

Setting Up a Wi-Fi Connection

If you're using a laptop or a desktop with Wi-Fi capability, you'll likely want to connect to a wireless network. Here's how you can set up a Wi-Fi connection in Windows 11:

1. Click on the **Start** button and select **Settings** (the gear-shaped icon).
2. In the Settings window, select **Network & Internet**.
3. Under the **Wi-Fi** category, you'll see the available wireless networks in your vicinity. Click on the network you want to connect to.
4. If the network is secured (as most are), you'll be prompted to enter the network's password. Enter the password and click **Connect**.

Windows 11 will attempt to connect to the selected Wi-Fi network, and once connected, it will be marked as "Connected" in the Wi-Fi settings.

Managing Wi-Fi Networks

Windows 11 allows you to manage your saved Wi-Fi networks and prioritize them. Here's how:

1. In the **Wi-Fi** settings, scroll down to the **Manage known networks** section.
2. Here, you'll see a list of all the Wi-Fi networks your device has connected to in the past.
3. To forget a network, click on it and then click **Forget**. This is useful for networks you no longer use or trust.
4. To change the priority of networks, click on a network and select **Move up** or **Move down** to change its position in the list. Windows prioritizes networks higher in the list when multiple known networks are available.

Setting Up an Ethernet Connection

If you're using a desktop computer or a laptop with an Ethernet port, you can set up a wired Ethernet connection. Here's how:

1. Plug one end of an Ethernet cable into your computer's Ethernet port and the other end into a network jack or router.
2. Windows 11 should automatically detect the Ethernet connection and establish it.

You can check the status of your Ethernet connection in the **Ethernet** section of the **Network & Internet** settings. It will display as "Connected" if the connection is successful.

Troubleshooting Network Connections

If you encounter issues with your Wi-Fi or Ethernet connection, Windows 11 provides built-in troubleshooting tools to help diagnose and resolve problems. To use the network troubleshooter:

1. In the **Network & Internet** settings, scroll down to the **Advanced network settings** section.
2. Click on **Network troubleshooter** to launch the troubleshooting tool.
3. Follow the on-screen instructions to identify and fix network-related issues.

Managing your Wi-Fi and Ethernet connections in Windows 11 is straightforward, and these steps should help you set up and troubleshoot your network connections effectively, ensuring a reliable internet and local network experience.

8.3. Sharing Files and Folders Over a Network

Sharing files and folders over a network is a common task for both home and business users. Windows 11 provides several methods to share files and folders with other devices on your network. In this section, we will explore how to set up file and folder sharing and manage shared resources.

Enabling File and Printer Sharing

Before you can share files and folders, you need to ensure that file and printer sharing is enabled on your Windows 11 computer. Here's how to do it:

1. Click on the **Start** button and select **Settings** (the gear-shaped icon).
2. In the Settings window, select **Network & Internet**.
3. Scroll down to the **Advanced network settings** section and click on **Sharing options**.
4. Under **Private** or **Guest or Public** (depending on your network type), ensure that **Turn on file and printer sharing** is enabled.

Sharing a Folder or File

Once file and printer sharing is enabled, you can share a folder or file with other users on your network:

1. Navigate to the folder or file you want to share in File Explorer.
2. Right-click on the folder or file and select **Properties**.
3. In the Properties window, go to the **Sharing** tab.
4. Click on the **Share** button.

You can choose which users or groups to share the folder or file with and set their permission level (Read or Read/Write). You can also use the **Add** button to add more users or groups.

Accessing Shared Files and Folders

On other devices connected to the same network, you can access shared files and folders as follows:

1. Open File Explorer on the remote device.
2. In the left sidebar, under **Network**, you should see your Windows 11 computer listed. Click on it to access shared resources.
3. You'll see the shared folders and files. Double-click on a shared resource to access its contents.

Mapping Network Drives

If you frequently access shared resources, you can map them as network drives for easy access:

1. In File Explorer on the remote device, click **This PC** in the left sidebar.
2. Click on **Computer** in the top menu.
3. Select **Map network drive**.
4. Choose a drive letter for the network drive and specify the folder path (e.g.,).
5. Click **Finish**.

The network drive will now appear in File Explorer, allowing you to access shared resources more conveniently.

Advanced Sharing Settings

To further customize your sharing settings, you can access advanced sharing options:

1. In the **Sharing options** (as mentioned earlier), click on **Change advanced sharing settings**.
2. Here, you can customize settings such as network discovery, file and printer sharing, and public folder sharing. Adjust these settings according to your network requirements.

Remember that while sharing files and folders over a network can be convenient, it's essential to manage permissions and security settings carefully to ensure that only authorized users have access to your shared resources. Regularly review and update sharing permissions to maintain network security.

8.4. Troubleshooting Common Network Issues

Network issues can be frustrating, but they are a common part of using computers in a connected world. Windows 11 offers several tools and techniques to diagnose and troubleshoot network problems. In this section, we will explore common network issues and how to resolve them.

1. No Internet Connection

- **Solution**: First, check if other devices on the same network have internet access. If they do, the issue may be with your computer. Try rebooting your modem and router. If that doesn't work, open the **Network & Internet** settings, run the **Network troubleshooter**, and follow the suggested fixes.

2. Limited or No Connectivity

- **Solution**: This often occurs when your computer can connect to the network but not the internet. Verify that your router and modem are functioning correctly. Try restarting them. You can also try releasing and renewing your IP address using the Command Prompt. Open Command Prompt as an administrator and type the following commands:

```
ipconfig /release
ipconfig /renew
```

3. Slow Internet Speed

- **Solution**: Slow internet can result from various factors. Ensure that no other devices or applications are using excessive bandwidth. Run an internet speed test to check if your connection meets your subscribed speed. If it doesn't, contact your internet service provider.

4. Wi-Fi Connectivity Issues

- **Solution**: If you're experiencing Wi-Fi issues, try disconnecting and reconnecting to the Wi-Fi network. Ensure that you're within the Wi-Fi range. If problems persist, try resetting your Wi-Fi adapter by right-clicking on it in **Device Manager** and selecting **Disable**, then **Enable**.

5. Cannot Access Network Shares

- **Solution**: If you can't access shared folders or resources on your network, check the following:
    - Ensure that the shared resource is online and accessible.
    - Verify that you have the necessary permissions to access the shared resource.
    - Check your network settings, including DNS and gateway settings.
    - Try accessing the resource by IP address instead of hostname.

6. Network Printer Not Working

- **Solution**: If your network printer is not working, ensure that it's turned on and connected to the network. Verify that the printer drivers are correctly installed on your computer. You can also try removing and re-adding the printer in **Devices and Printers**.

7. DNS Resolution Issues

- **Solution**: If you're having trouble accessing websites by their domain names, it could be a DNS issue. Try changing your DNS server settings to use a different DNS provider, such as Google DNS (8.8.8.8 and 8.8.4.4) or Cloudflare DNS (1.1.1.1 and 1.0.0.1).

8. Firewall or Security Software Blocking Connections

- **Solution**: Sometimes, firewall or security software can block network connections. Check your firewall settings and ensure that the necessary exceptions or rules are in place for your network services and applications.

9. Network Card Driver Issues

- **Solution**: Outdated or corrupted network card drivers can cause network problems. Check for driver updates in **Device Manager** and update your network card drivers if needed.

10. Network Hardware Failures

- **Solution**: If none of the above solutions work, there could be a hardware issue with your modem, router, or network card. In such cases, you may need to contact your hardware manufacturer for assistance or consider replacing the faulty hardware.

Remember that troubleshooting network issues may require some technical expertise, and it's crucial to be cautious when making changes to network settings. If you're unsure about a specific troubleshooting step, seek assistance from a knowledgeable friend or a professional to avoid making the problem worse. Additionally, always back up important data before attempting significant network configuration changes.

8.5. Using Remote Desktop and VPN for Remote Access

In an increasingly interconnected world, the ability to access your computer or network remotely can be a valuable asset. Whether you need to work from home, manage a server in a data center, or assist a family member with computer issues from afar, Windows 11 provides two primary solutions for remote access: Remote Desktop and VPN (Virtual Private Network).

1. Remote Desktop

Remote Desktop is a built-in Windows feature that allows you to connect to another computer over a network or the internet as if you were sitting in front of it. To set up and use Remote Desktop:

1. **Enable Remote Desktop**: On the computer you want to connect to, go to **Settings > System > Remote Desktop**, and enable the **Remote Desktop** toggle. Note down the computer's name or IP address.

2. **Connect from Another Computer**: On the computer you're connecting from, open the **Remote Desktop** app (you can search for it in the Start menu). Enter the name or IP address of the target computer and click **Connect**.

3. **Log In**: You'll be prompted to enter the username and password of the target computer. Once entered, you'll gain remote access to the desktop.

4. **Customize Remote Desktop Settings**: You can configure various settings like display quality, resource redirection, and more in the Remote Desktop app's options.

Remember that for Remote Desktop to work, both the target and source computers need to be running Windows Pro, Enterprise, or Education editions. Additionally, the target computer must have Remote Desktop enabled, and you need the appropriate credentials to log in.

2. VPN (Virtual Private Network)

A VPN creates a secure, encrypted connection between your computer and a remote network or server. This allows you to access resources on the remote network as if you were physically present there. Here's how to set up and use a VPN in Windows 11:

1. **Choose a VPN Service**: Subscribe to a reputable VPN service. There are many VPN providers available, each with its own features and pricing.

2. **Install the VPN Client**: Download and install the VPN client provided by your chosen VPN service on your Windows 11 computer.

3. **Connect to the VPN**: Launch the VPN client, log in with your credentials, and connect to a VPN server of your choice. Once connected, your internet traffic is encrypted and routed through the VPN server.

4. **Access Remote Resources**: With the VPN connected, you can access resources on the remote network, such as shared files, servers, or devices. These resources will appear as if they are on your local network.

5. **Disconnect**: When you're done using the VPN, simply disconnect from the VPN server through the VPN client.

VPN is a versatile tool used for various purposes, including securing your internet connection on public Wi-Fi, accessing geo-restricted content, and ensuring privacy. It's essential to choose a reliable VPN service that fits your needs.

Keep in mind that both Remote Desktop and VPN should be used securely. Ensure strong passwords, keep your systems updated with security patches, and use these tools responsibly and ethically. Always follow best practices for remote access to protect your data and network.

Chapter 9: Advanced Customization and Tweaks

In this chapter, we will explore advanced customization and tweaks that allow you to tailor your Windows 11 experience to your specific preferences and needs. Windows 11 provides various tools and settings that go beyond the basics of personalization and system configuration. Whether you're looking to fine-tune your user interface, optimize performance for gaming or creative work, or make advanced adjustments to power management and virtual desktops, this chapter covers it all.

9.1. Exploring the Windows Registry for Advanced Customization

The Windows Registry is a central database that stores configuration settings and options for the Windows operating system and installed applications. It contains a vast array of keys and values that control various aspects of the system's behavior. While it's a powerful tool for customization, it's essential to approach it with caution, as making incorrect changes can lead to system instability or even failure. Here's how to explore and use the Windows Registry for advanced customization:

Accessing the Windows Registry Editor

1. **Open the Run Dialog**: Press Win + R to open the Run dialog.

2. **Launch Registry Editor**: Type regedit into the Run dialog and press Enter. This will open the Windows Registry Editor.

Navigating the Registry

- The Registry is organized into a hierarchical structure similar to a file system, with keys and subkeys. The top-level keys are called "Hives."

- Common Hives include HKEY_CLASSES_ROOT, HKEY_CURRENT_USER, HKEY_LOCAL_MACHINE, HKEY_USERS, and HKEY_CURRENT_CONFIG.

- Navigate through the Registry by expanding these keys and their subkeys. Be cautious not to make changes unless you're certain about their purpose.

Making Changes

- Before making any changes, it's essential to back up the Registry. In the Registry Editor, go to File > Export and save a copy of the Registry to a safe location.

- To modify a value, double-click on it, make your changes, and click OK. Ensure you understand the implications of your changes.

Customization Examples

1. **Taskbar and Start Menu**: You can customize the Taskbar's appearance and behavior, including its size, location, and pinned items, by navigating to HKEY_CURRENT_USER\Software\Microsoft\Windows\CurrentVersion\Explorer\Advanced.

2. **Disable Windows Defender**: While not recommended for security reasons, you can find options related to Windows Defender at `HKEY_LOCAL_MACHINE\SOFTWARE\Policies\Microsoft\Windows Defender`.

3. **Advanced Power Settings**: Adjust advanced power settings beyond what's available in the Control Panel by exploring `HKEY_LOCAL_MACHINE\SYSTEM\CurrentControlSet\Control\Power`.

4. **Visual Effects**: Fine-tune visual effects to optimize performance or aesthetics at `HKEY_CURRENT_USER\Software\Microsoft\Windows\CurrentVersion\Explorer\VisualEffects`.

Remember that making changes in the Registry carries risks, and it's advisable to research and backup before proceeding. It's also worth noting that some advanced customization options may not be available in Windows Home editions, as certain Registry keys are restricted.

In this chapter, we'll explore more customization and optimization options, including Taskbar and Start Menu tweaks, advanced graphic settings, power management, and virtual desktops. These advanced customizations can help you tailor Windows 11 to your specific needs and preferences, making it a more efficient and personalized operating system.

9.2. Customizing the Taskbar and Start Menu for Efficiency

Customizing the Taskbar and Start Menu is a great way to enhance your Windows 11 experience. These elements are central to your daily interactions with the operating system, so tailoring them to your preferences can boost productivity. In this section, we'll explore various ways to customize the Taskbar and Start Menu for efficiency.

Taskbar Customization

1. *Taskbar Placement*: You can move the Taskbar to different edges of the screen—bottom, left, or right. Right-click on an empty area of the Taskbar, go to "Taskbar settings," and under "Taskbar behaviors," choose your preferred position.

2. *Taskbar Size*: Adjust the Taskbar's height by dragging its upper edge. Make it smaller to save screen space or larger for more visibility.

3. *Pin Apps*: Pin frequently used apps to the Taskbar for quick access. Right-click on an app in the Start Menu and select "Pin to Taskbar."

4. *Taskbar Icons*: Customize which icons appear on the Taskbar. Right-click on the Taskbar, choose "Taskbar settings," and scroll down to "Notification area." Click "Select which icons appear on the taskbar" to manage visibility.

5. *Taskbar Toolbars*: Add toolbars to the Taskbar for easy access to specific folders or functions. Right-click on the Taskbar, hover over "Toolbars," and select from available options.

Start Menu Customization

6. *Live Tiles*: The Start Menu features Live Tiles that can display real-time information. You can resize, rearrange, or remove Live Tiles to suit your preferences. Right-click on a Live Tile and select the desired option.

7. *App Groups*: Organize apps into groups for a cleaner Start Menu. Drag and drop app icons to create groups, or use the "Pin to Start" option to add apps to existing groups.

8. *Start Menu Folders*: Customize the Start Menu by adding or removing folders. Right-click on the Start button and select "Settings" > "Personalization" > "Start." Use the "Choose which folders appear on Start" option to configure folder visibility.

9. *Search Bar*: Adjust the visibility of the Search bar in the Start Menu. Right-click on the Taskbar, choose "Taskbar settings," and scroll down to "Search." Customize the Search bar's appearance and behavior.

10. *Start Menu Background*: Personalize the Start Menu background by going to "Settings" > "Personalization" > "Colors." Enable the "Start, taskbar, and action center" option to set a custom background color or image.

Keyboard Shortcuts

11. *Quick Access*: Use keyboard shortcuts to navigate the Taskbar and Start Menu efficiently. Press Win to open the Start Menu, and press Win + [Number] to launch or switch to a pinned app on the Taskbar (e.g., Win + 1 for the first app).

12. *Search*: Press Win + S to open the Windows Search bar, allowing you to quickly search for apps, files, and settings directly from the Start Menu.

By customizing the Taskbar and Start Menu to align with your workflow and preferences, you can streamline your daily tasks and make Windows 11 more efficient and user-friendly. These customization options allow you to create a computing environment that suits your unique needs.

9.3. Advanced Graphic Settings for Gamers and Designers

In Windows 11, advanced graphic settings offer a wealth of options for both gamers and graphic designers. These settings allow you to optimize your system's performance, enhance visual quality, and customize graphics-related configurations. In this section, we will delve into various aspects of advanced graphic settings.

Graphics Control Panel

1. **Graphics Control Panel**: Access the Graphics Control Panel for your GPU, whether it's from NVIDIA, AMD, or Intel. You can typically access it by right-clicking on the desktop and selecting the GPU control panel option. Here, you can configure various graphics-related settings.

Resolution and Scaling

2. **Resolution**: Adjust your display resolution to balance between visual quality and performance. Higher resolutions offer sharper visuals, while lower ones may boost FPS in games. Right-click on the desktop, go to "Display settings," and select your desired resolution under "Display resolution."

3. **Scaling**: Modify scaling settings to make content larger or smaller on your screen. This can be beneficial for high-resolution displays or accessibility purposes. In "Display settings," under "Scale and layout," adjust the scaling options.

Graphics Performance

4. **Graphics Performance Preference**: Windows 11 offers a Graphics Performance Preference feature. You can specify which apps should prioritize graphics performance. Go to "Settings" > "System" > "Advanced" > "Graphics settings" to configure this option.

5. **Hardware-Accelerated GPU Scheduling**: If your GPU and drivers support it, enable Hardware-Accelerated GPU Scheduling for potentially improved performance. In "Settings," navigate to "System" > "Display" > "Graphics settings" and enable this feature.

Gaming Enhancements

6. **Game Mode**: Activate Game Mode to optimize system resources for gaming. Press Win + G to open the Game Bar, where you can enable Game Mode for specific games.

7. **Auto HDR**: If you have a compatible display and GPU, Auto HDR can enhance the visual experience in supported games. Check the "Windows HD Color settings" in "Display settings" to enable Auto HDR.

8. **FPS Counter**: Monitor your game's performance with the built-in FPS counter. To enable it, open the Game Bar (Win + G) and go to "Performance" settings.

Color Calibration

9. **Color Calibration**: Fine-tune color settings for your display by calibrating it. Search for "Calibrate display color" in the Start Menu and follow the on-screen instructions to adjust gamma, brightness, contrast, and color balance.

Multiple Displays

10. **Multiple Displays**: *If you use multiple monitors, customize their arrangement, resolution, and orientation in "Display settings." You can also set a primary display and choose how taskbars and notifications work across screens.*

Graphics Driver Updates

11. **Graphics Driver Updates**: *Regularly update your graphics drivers to ensure compatibility, performance improvements, and bug fixes. Visit your GPU manufacturer's website or use their driver update tool for the latest drivers.*

Graphic Design Software

12. **Graphic Design Software Optimization**: *Graphic designers can optimize their design software for better performance. In most graphic design applications, you can adjust settings related to rendering, canvas size, and GPU acceleration.*

DirectX and GPU Features

13. **DirectX Version**: *Check which DirectX version your system uses. DirectX 12 provides better graphics performance in modern games. You can verify this in the "System Information" utility (Win + R, type dxdiag, and press Enter).*

14. **Ray Tracing and DLSS**: *If your GPU supports ray tracing and DLSS (Deep Learning Super Sampling), explore games that utilize these features for realistic visuals and improved performance.*

By exploring and configuring these advanced graphic settings, you can fine-tune your Windows 11 experience to meet the demands of gaming, graphic design, or any graphics-intensive tasks you may encounter. These options empower you to strike the right balance between performance and visual quality, ensuring a smooth and enjoyable computing experience.

9.4. Power Management and Advanced Battery Settings

Efficient power management is crucial, whether you're using a laptop on the go or a desktop PC. Windows 11 provides a range of advanced battery settings and power management options to help you extend battery life and optimize power usage. In this section, we'll explore these settings and how to make the most of them.

Power Plans

1. **Power Plans**: *Windows 11 offers various power plans, such as Balanced, Power Saver, and High Performance. These plans control the system's power usage and performance. To select a power plan, right-click the battery icon in the taskbar and choose "Power & sleep settings." Click on "Additional power settings" to view and select the available plans.*

2. **Custom Power Plans**: *You can create custom power plans to tailor settings to your specific needs. In the "Power & sleep settings," click "Create a power plan" on the left panel. Customize the plan's settings, including screen brightness, sleep timers, and more.*

Battery Saver

3. **Battery Saver**: *Battery Saver mode reduces background processes and screen brightness to conserve battery life. You can manually enable it by clicking on the battery icon in the taskbar and selecting "Battery saver." To configure Battery Saver settings, go to "Settings" > "System" > "Power & sleep" > "Additional power settings."*

Advanced Battery Settings

4. **Advanced Battery Settings**: *Access advanced battery settings by clicking on "Change plan settings" next to your selected power plan. Here, you can configure options like when the screen turns off, when the computer sleeps, and the behavior of the power button and lid.*

5. **Processor Power Management**: *Customize how your processor manages power. You can set minimum and maximum processor states, which can affect performance and power consumption. To do this, click "Change advanced power settings" in the advanced battery settings and navigate to the "Processor power management" section.*

Sleep Settings

6. **Sleep Settings**: *Adjust sleep settings to strike a balance between saving power and convenience. You can specify when your computer sleeps or turns off the display. These settings are available in the advanced battery settings under "Sleep."*

Lid Closing Action

7. **Lid Closing Action**: *For laptop users, configure what happens when you close the laptop lid. You can set it to sleep, hibernate, or do nothing. To change this setting, go to the advanced battery settings and find "Lid close action."*

Background Apps

8. **Background Apps**: *Manage which apps are allowed to run in the background. Go to "Settings" > "Privacy" > "Background apps" to control which apps can consume power when not in use.*

Battery Report

*9. **Battery Report**: Generate a battery report to monitor your battery's health and usage. Open Command Prompt as an administrator and type powercfg /batteryreport to generate a battery report in HTML format. This report provides valuable information about your battery's capacity and charge cycles.*

Dynamic Tick

*10. **Dynamic Tick**: Windows 11 uses dynamic tick by default, which adjusts the timer tick rate to conserve power when the system is idle. This feature is automatic and doesn't require user configuration.*

Power Efficiency Diagnostics

*11. **Power Efficiency Diagnostics**: Windows includes a built-in tool to diagnose power efficiency issues. Open Command Prompt as an administrator and type powercfg /energy to generate an energy efficiency report. This report can help identify power-hungry components or settings.*

Battery Care (Laptops)

*12. **Battery Care (Laptops)**: Some laptops come with battery care features that limit charging to a certain percentage to extend battery lifespan. Check your laptop manufacturer's utility or settings for battery care options.*

By fine-tuning these power management and advanced battery settings in Windows 11, you can significantly impact your device's battery life and power efficiency. Whether you're using a laptop or a desktop, optimizing power settings ensures a balance between performance and energy conservation, resulting in a more efficient and eco-friendly computing experience.

9.5. Utilizing Virtual Desktops for Enhanced Productivity

Virtual desktops are a powerful feature in Windows 11 that can significantly enhance your productivity by allowing you to organize and switch between multiple desktop environments seamlessly. In this section, we will explore how to utilize virtual desktops effectively.

Creating and Managing Virtual Desktops

1. **Create a Virtual Desktop**: To create a new virtual desktop, press Windows Key + Tab or click the Task View icon on the taskbar. Then, click the "New Desktop" button at the top left. You can also use the shortcut Ctrl + Windows Key + D to create a new desktop quickly.

2. **Switch Between Desktops**: To switch between virtual desktops, press Windows Key + Tab, then click on the desktop you want to switch to. Alternatively, use the

keyboard shortcuts `Ctrl + Windows Key + Left Arrow` or `Ctrl + Windows Key + Right Arrow` to cycle through desktops.

3. **Move Apps Between Desktops**: Open Task View, hover over the app you want to move, right-click, and select "Move to" to choose the target desktop.

4. **Close Virtual Desktops**: To close a virtual desktop, open Task View, hover over the desktop you want to close, and click the "X" button that appears.

Organizing Your Workspaces

5. **Customize Desktops**: You can customize each virtual desktop to suit different tasks. For example, you can have one desktop for work-related apps and another for leisure or personal tasks. This separation helps you stay organized.

6. **Name Your Desktops**: Give your virtual desktops meaningful names to make it easier to identify their purpose. Right-click on the desktop thumbnail in Task View and select "Rename."

Keyboard Shortcuts

7. **Keyboard Shortcuts**: Windows 11 offers several keyboard shortcuts to manage virtual desktops efficiently. Here are some useful ones:
   - `Windows Key + Ctrl + D`: Create a new virtual desktop.
   - `Windows Key + Ctrl + F4`: Close the current virtual desktop.
   - `Windows Key + Ctrl + Left Arrow`: Switch to the virtual desktop on the left.
   - `Windows Key + Ctrl + Right Arrow`: Switch to the virtual desktop on the right.
   - `Windows Key + Ctrl + Number`: Switch to a specific virtual desktop by its corresponding number (e.g., 1 for the first desktop, 2 for the second).

Taskbar and Alt + Tab

8. **Taskbar Integration**: The taskbar displays open apps from all virtual desktops, making it easy to access your running applications regardless of the desktop they're on.

9. **Alt + Tab**: When you press `Alt + Tab`, you can cycle through open apps across all virtual desktops. This is a quick way to switch between applications.

Multitasking and Productivity

10. **Multitasking**: Virtual desktops enable efficient multitasking. You can have different projects or tasks on separate desktops, minimizing clutter and distractions.

11. **Presentation and Focus**: Use virtual desktops when presenting or working on specific tasks that require concentration. You can keep your work-related apps on one desktop and personal apps on another, reducing the risk of distraction.

12. **Hotkeys and Navigation**: Familiarize yourself with the hotkeys and navigation shortcuts for virtual desktops to become more efficient in managing your workspaces.

Virtual desktops in Windows 11 are a valuable tool for enhancing productivity and organizing your workflow. By creating multiple desktops tailored to different tasks or projects, you can reduce clutter, streamline your work, and switch between contexts effortlessly. Mastering virtual desktops is a skill that can significantly boost your efficiency and make multitasking a breeze.

10.1. Introduction to Command Prompt and PowerShell

In Windows 11, the Command Prompt and PowerShell are powerful command-line interfaces that provide advanced control over your system, files, and tasks. Whether you're a seasoned IT professional or a curious user, these command-line tools offer a range of capabilities. This section introduces you to the basics of Command Prompt and PowerShell.

Command Prompt

Accessing Command Prompt
1. **Opening Command Prompt**: You can open the Command Prompt in several ways:
    -   Press Windows Key + S, type "Command Prompt," and select it from the search results.
    -   Press Windows Key + X and choose "Windows Terminal (Admin)" to open it with administrative privileges.
    -   Use the Windows Key + R shortcut, type "cmd," and press Enter.

Basic Commands
2. **Navigating Folders**: Use cd (change directory) to navigate through folders. For example, cd Documents moves to the "Documents" folder.

3. **Listing Files and Folders**: The dir command lists the files and folders in the current directory.

4. **Creating and Removing Directories**: You can create directories with mkdir (make directory) and remove them with rmdir (remove directory).

5. **Copying and Moving Files**: copy and move are used to copy and move files, respectively.

6. **Executing Programs**: You can run programs or open files by typing their names and pressing Enter.

PowerShell

Accessing PowerShell
7. **Opening PowerShell**: Similarly, you can open PowerShell:
    -   Search for "PowerShell" and select it.
    -   Open "Windows Terminal (Admin)" for administrative access.
    -   Use the Run dialog (Windows Key + R) and type "powershell."

PowerShell Basics
8. **Cmdlets**: PowerShell uses cmdlets (pronounced "command-lets") for its commands. Cmdlets are small, single-function commands like Get-Process or Set-Item.

9. **Pipelines**: PowerShell excels in its ability to chain cmdlets together using pipelines (`|`). For example, `Get-Service | Where-Object { $_.Status -eq 'Running' }` retrieves running services.

10. **Variables**: You can create and use variables in PowerShell. To assign a value to a variable, use `$variableName = value`.

11. **Scripting**: PowerShell allows you to write and run scripts. Save your script with a `.ps1` extension, and execute it by typing its filename.

12. **Remote Management**: PowerShell enables remote management of computers using technologies like PowerShell Remoting.

Transitioning from Command Prompt to PowerShell

13. **PowerShell as the Future**: While Command Prompt commands still work in Windows 11, Microsoft encourages transitioning to PowerShell, which offers more advanced features and compatibility with modern Windows technologies.

14. **Command Aliases**: Many Command Prompt commands have aliases in PowerShell, making the transition easier. For example, `dir` is an alias for `Get-ChildItem`.

15. **Learning Resources**: To dive deeper into Command Prompt and PowerShell, explore Microsoft's official documentation and online tutorials. These resources will help you become proficient in both tools.

Both Command Prompt and PowerShell have their strengths, and learning to use them effectively can enhance your Windows 11 experience. While Command Prompt remains a valuable tool for quick tasks and familiarity, PowerShell's versatility, scripting capabilities, and compatibility with modern Windows technologies make it a powerful choice for advanced users and IT professionals. Understanding both tools equips you with the skills needed to navigate and control your Windows 11 system efficiently.

10.2. Basic Command Line Operations and Shortcuts

In this section, we will explore some fundamental command line operations and shortcuts that will help you become more proficient in using the Command Prompt and PowerShell in Windows 11.

1. Command Auto-Completion

Both Command Prompt and PowerShell support command auto-completion. Pressing the Tab key while typing a command or file/folder path will auto-complete the command or path if it's unique. If there are multiple possibilities, pressing Tab twice will display a list of available options.

2. Navigating Directories

Changing Drives
- In the Command Prompt, you can change drives directly by typing the drive letter followed by a colon (e.g., `D:`).
- In PowerShell, use `Set-Location` or its alias `cd` to change drives (e.g., `cd D:\`).

Navigate to User Profile
- Use `cd` or `Set-Location` followed by the tilde (~) to quickly navigate to your user profile directory (e.g., `cd ~`).

Go Up One Directory
- To move up one level in the directory hierarchy, use `cd ..` in both Command Prompt and PowerShell.

3. Repeating Previous Commands

Command Prompt
- In the Command Prompt, you can quickly repeat the previous command by pressing the `Up Arrow` key.

PowerShell
- In PowerShell, you can also use the `Up Arrow` key to recall previous commands. Additionally, you can use `Get-History` to view a list of recent commands and `Invoke-History` to execute a specific command from the history.

4. Clearing the Screen

Command Prompt
- To clear the screen in the Command Prompt, simply type `cls` and press `Enter`.

PowerShell
- In PowerShell, use the `Clear-Host` cmdlet to clear the screen.

5. Copying and Pasting
- You can copy text from your Windows 11 environment and paste it into the Command Prompt or PowerShell by using the `Ctrl + C` and `Ctrl + V` keyboard shortcuts, respectively.

6. Running Programs with Elevated Privileges
- In both Command Prompt and PowerShell, you can run a program with administrative privileges by right-clicking on the respective application (e.g., Command Prompt or PowerShell) and selecting "Run as administrator." This allows you to execute commands that require elevated permissions.

7. Using Wildcards

- Both Command Prompt and PowerShell support wildcards (* and ?) for pattern matching. For example, *.txt will match all .txt files in a directory, and file?.txt will match files like file1.txt and fileA.txt.

8. Redirecting Output

- You can redirect the output of a command to a file using the > symbol. For example, dir > filelist.txt will save the directory listing to a file named filelist.txt.

9. Running Multiple Commands

- In both environments, you can run multiple commands sequentially by separating them with &. For example, command1 & command2 will execute command1, followed by command2.

10. Command Help

- Use the /? switch with a command to display its built-in help documentation. For example, dir /? will show the options and usage of the dir command.

Mastering these basic command line operations and shortcuts will make you more efficient when working with the Command Prompt and PowerShell in Windows 11. As you become more comfortable, you can explore advanced commands and scripting to automate tasks and customize your command line experience further.

10.3. Automating Tasks with Batch Files and Scripts

In this section, we'll delve into the world of batch files and scripts to automate tasks and streamline your workflow in both Command Prompt and PowerShell on Windows 11.

Batch Files

Batch files, also known as batch scripts or .bat files, are sequences of commands that are executed in a batch (one after the other). These files can automate repetitive tasks, simplify complex operations, and save time.

Creating a Batch File

To create a batch file:

1. Open a text editor like Notepad.
2. Write your batch commands one line at a time.
3. Save the file with a .bat extension (e.g., my_script.bat).

Basic Batch Commands

- echo: Display text on the screen.

- `cd`: Change the current directory.
- `dir`: List files and directories.
- `copy`: Copy files and directories.
- `del`: Delete files and directories.
- `move`: Move or rename files and directories.

Example Batch File

```
@echo off
echo Welcome to My Batch Script
cd C:\MyFolder
dir
copy file.txt D:\Backup
echo Task Completed
```

Running a Batch File

To execute a batch file, simply double-click it, or open a Command Prompt and type the batch file's name followed by `.bat`. For example, if the file is named `my_script.bat`, you would run `my_script.bat`.

PowerShell Scripts

PowerShell scripts are more versatile and powerful than batch files. They allow you to leverage the full capabilities of PowerShell to automate complex tasks, work with data, and interact with the Windows operating system.

Creating a PowerShell Script

To create a PowerShell script:

1. Open a text editor like Notepad.
2. Write your PowerShell commands and script logic.
3. Save the file with a .ps1 extension (e.g., `my_script.ps1`).

Basic PowerShell Commands

- `Write-Host`: Display text on the screen.
- `Set-Location` (or `cd`): Change the current location (directory).
- `Get-ChildItem` (or `dir`): List files and directories.
- `Copy-Item`: Copy files and directories.
- `Remove-Item`: Delete files and directories.
- `Move-Item`: Move or rename files and directories.

Example PowerShell Script

```
Write-Host "Welcome to My PowerShell Script"
Set-Location C:\MyFolder
Get-ChildItem
Copy-Item file.txt D:\Backup
Write-Host "Task Completed"
```

To execute a PowerShell script, open PowerShell and use the `.\` prefix followed by the script's name. For example, if the script is named `my_script.ps1`, you would run `.\my_script.ps1`.

Automation Benefits

Both batch files and PowerShell scripts offer significant automation benefits, including:

- Time-saving: Automate repetitive tasks to reduce manual work.
- Consistency: Ensure tasks are performed consistently without human error.
- Efficiency: Streamline complex operations into simple scripts.
- Customization: Tailor scripts to your specific needs.
- Productivity: Free up your time for more important tasks.

As you become more familiar with batch files and PowerShell scripts, you can explore advanced scripting techniques, interact with external data sources, and create sophisticated automation solutions to enhance your Windows 11 experience.

10.4. Advanced PowerShell Commands and Scripting

In this section, we'll dive into advanced PowerShell commands and scripting techniques to help you harness the full power of automation in Windows 11.

1. Functions and Modules

One of the fundamental concepts in PowerShell scripting is the use of functions and modules. Functions allow you to encapsulate a set of commands into a reusable block of code, making your scripts more organized and maintainable. Modules are collections of functions and variables that can be easily shared and imported into your scripts.

Here's an example of defining a simple function in PowerShell:

```
function Say-Hello {
    param (
        [string]$Name
    )
    Write-Host "Hello, $Name!"
}

# Call the function
Say-Hello -Name "John"
```

2. Error Handling

Effective error handling is crucial in scripting. PowerShell provides mechanisms to catch and handle errors gracefully. The `try`, `catch`, and `finally` blocks allow you to control what happens when an error occurs. For example:

```
try {
    # Attempt an operation that may generate an error
    Get-Content -Path "NonExistentFile.txt"
}
catch {
    # Handle the error
    Write-Host "An error occurred: $_"
}
finally {
    # Code in this block runs regardless of whether there was an error
    Write-Host "Cleanup or final actions here"
}
```

3. Remote Script Execution

PowerShell enables you to run scripts on remote computers. The `Invoke-Command` cmdlet allows you to execute commands or scripts on remote machines, making it a powerful tool for managing and automating tasks across a network.

```
# Execute a command on a remote computer
Invoke-Command -ComputerName "RemoteComputer" -ScriptBlock { Get-Process }
```

4. Scheduled Tasks

You can use PowerShell to create and manage scheduled tasks. The `New-ScheduledTaskTrigger` and `Register-ScheduledTask` cmdlets allow you to schedule scripts to run at specific times or intervals.

```
# Create a scheduled task that runs a script daily
$Trigger = New-ScheduledTaskTrigger -Daily -At "3:00 AM"
Register-ScheduledTask -Action { Invoke-Expression -Command "C:\Scripts\MyScr
ipt.ps1" } -Trigger $Trigger -TaskName "DailyScript"
```

5. Desired State Configuration (DSC)

PowerShell Desired State Configuration is a powerful feature for ensuring that your systems are configured as desired and remain in the desired state. You define configurations using PowerShell scripts, and DSC ensures that systems comply with those configurations.

```
# Define a DSC configuration
Configuration MyConfiguration {
    Node "localhost" {
        WindowsFeature IIS {
            Ensure = "Present"
```

```
            Name = "Web-Server"
        }
    }
}
```

```
# Apply the configuration
MyConfiguration
Start-DscConfiguration -Path .\MyConfiguration -Wait -Verbose
```

6. Working with JSON and REST APIs

PowerShell excels at working with structured data like JSON. You can use `ConvertTo-Json` and `ConvertFrom-Json` cmdlets to interact with JSON data. Additionally, PowerShell can make HTTP requests to REST APIs using `Invoke-RestMethod`.

```
# Fetch data from a REST API
$response = Invoke-RestMethod -Uri "https://api.example.com/data"
$response | ConvertTo-Json | Set-Content -Path "data.json"
```

By mastering these advanced PowerShell techniques, you can create robust and efficient automation scripts that tackle complex tasks, interact with external systems, and help you manage your Windows 11 environment effectively.

10.5. Managing System Resources and Services via Command Line

In this section, we will explore how to manage system resources and services using command-line tools in Windows 11. Command-line tools offer a powerful way to control and monitor various aspects of your system without relying on graphical interfaces.

1. Task Manager (tasklist and taskkill)

The `tasklist` command allows you to view a list of running processes on your system. You can filter the list and get detailed information about each process. For example, to list all running processes, open Command Prompt or PowerShell and run:

```
tasklist
```

To terminate a specific process, you can use the `taskkill` command. You'll need to provide either the process name or its process ID (PID). For example, to end a process with the name "notepad.exe," run:

```
taskkill /F /IM notepad.exe
```

2. Resource Monitor (resmon)

Resource Monitor provides an in-depth view of your system's resource usage, including CPU, memory, disk, and network. To open Resource Monitor, press `Win + R`, type "resmon," and press Enter. You can also launch it from the command line:

```
resmon
```

3. System Information (systeminfo)

The `systeminfo` command provides a comprehensive report on your system's configuration, including hardware details, OS information, and more. To generate a system information report, simply run:

```
systeminfo
```

4. Services (sc and net)

You can manage Windows services from the command line using `sc` (Service Control) and `net` commands. For example, to start the "Print Spooler" service, run:

```
sc start spooler
```

To stop the service, replace "start" with "stop." Similarly, you can use the `net` command to start and stop services:

```
net start spooler
net stop spooler
```

5. Disk Management (diskpart)

The `diskpart` utility allows you to manage disks, partitions, and volumes. Use caution when working with `diskpart` as it can modify your disk configuration. To launch `diskpart`, open Command Prompt or PowerShell and run:

```
diskpart
```

6. Performance Monitor (perfmon)

Performance Monitor is a tool for tracking system performance over time. You can create custom performance counters and view real-time graphs. To open Performance Monitor, run:

```
perfmon
```

7. Windows Update (wusa)

The `wusa` (Windows Update Standalone Installer) command allows you to install or uninstall Windows updates manually. You'll need the path to the update file in CAB or MSU format. To install an update, run:

```
wusa C:\Path\To\Update.msu
```

These command-line tools provide advanced control over system resources, services, and system information. Whether you're troubleshooting issues, optimizing performance, or managing services, the command line is a versatile and efficient way to interact with your Windows 11 environment.

Chapter 11: Security and Maintenance

Section 11.1: Keeping Windows 11 Secure: Updates and Patches

In the ever-evolving landscape of cybersecurity, keeping your Windows 11 operating system up-to-date is paramount. Windows updates and patches play a pivotal role in maintaining the security and stability of your system. This section will delve into the importance of updates, how to configure update settings, and best practices for staying protected.

The Significance of Updates

Windows updates are not just about adding new features or improving the user interface; they are primarily focused on addressing security vulnerabilities and fixing software bugs. Cybercriminals are constantly searching for weaknesses in operating systems, and when they find one, they can exploit it to gain unauthorized access to your computer or steal your data. Updates are Microsoft's way of plugging these security holes and ensuring your system remains resilient.

Configuring Update Settings

Windows 11 provides flexibility in how you receive updates. You can configure your update settings to suit your needs while ensuring your system's security.

Automatic Updates

By default, Windows 11 is set to automatically download and install updates. This is the recommended option for most users, as it ensures that critical security updates are applied promptly. To check your update settings, go to **Settings** > **Windows Update** > **Advanced options**. Here, you can review and customize your update preferences.

Active Hours

You can specify "active hours," which are the times when you typically use your computer. During these hours, Windows will not automatically restart to apply updates, preventing interruptions when you need your device the most.

Pause Updates

Windows 11 allows you to pause updates for a limited time, providing you with control over when updates are installed. However, it's essential to resume updates promptly to maintain security.

Types of Updates

Microsoft releases several types of updates, each serving a specific purpose:

- **Security Updates:** These patches address vulnerabilities that could be exploited by malicious actors. Install them promptly to protect your system.

- **Quality Updates:** Quality updates include bug fixes and improvements to the operating system. While not directly related to security, they enhance the overall stability and performance of Windows.

- **Feature Updates:** Feature updates introduce new functionalities and improvements. They are usually released semi-annually and may require more significant installation time.

Best Practices

To ensure the security of your Windows 11 system, consider the following best practices:

1. **Regularly Check for Updates:** Even if you have automatic updates enabled, it's a good practice to periodically check for updates manually. Go to **Settings > Windows Update > Check for updates** to do this.

2. **Keep Third-Party Software Updated:** Windows updates cover the operating system and some Microsoft software. However, third-party applications can also pose security risks if not updated. Keep your browsers, plugins, and other software up-to-date.

3. **Backup Your Data:** While updates are designed to enhance security, there's always a small chance that something could go wrong during the update process. Regularly back up your important data to an external drive or cloud storage.

4. **Use Strong Passwords:** An updated operating system won't protect you from weak or easily guessable passwords. Ensure that your accounts are secured with strong, unique passwords.

5. **Enable Windows Defender:** Windows 11 comes with built-in antivirus protection called Windows Defender. Ensure it's enabled to provide an additional layer of security.

By following these practices and staying vigilant, you can keep your Windows 11 system secure and resilient to threats. Regular updates are a fundamental part of maintaining the overall health of your computer and safeguarding your digital life.

Section 11.2: Using Windows Defender and Third-Party Antivirus Software

When it comes to safeguarding your Windows 11 system against malware, viruses, and other online threats, you have several options. One of the primary built-in security tools in Windows 11 is Windows Defender, but there are also third-party antivirus solutions available. In this section, we will explore how to use Windows Defender effectively and discuss the considerations when choosing third-party antivirus software.

Windows Defender: Built-In Protection

Windows Defender, now known as **Microsoft Defender Antivirus**, comes pre-installed with Windows 11 and provides baseline protection against a wide range of threats. Here's how to make the most of it:

1. Real-Time Protection: Microsoft Defender Antivirus continuously monitors your system for malicious activity. Ensure that real-time protection is enabled by going to **Settings** > **Privacy & Security** > **Windows Security** > **Virus & threat protection**. Click on **Manage settings** and make sure "Real-time protection" is turned on.

2. Regular Scans: Microsoft Defender Antivirus also performs scheduled quick and full scans of your system. You can customize the scan schedule by going to **Settings** > **Privacy & Security** > **Windows Security** > **Virus & threat protection** > **Scan options**.

3. Windows Security Center: The **Windows Security** app centralizes various security features, including firewall settings, device performance, and account protection. Regularly review the security dashboard for important alerts and recommendations.

4. Tamper Protection: Enable "Tamper Protection" in Windows Security settings to prevent unauthorized changes to Microsoft Defender Antivirus settings. This adds an extra layer of security against malware attempting to disable your antivirus.

5. Cloud Protection: Microsoft Defender Antivirus utilizes cloud-based protection to identify and mitigate emerging threats. Ensure that "Cloud-delivered protection" is turned on in the settings.

Third-Party Antivirus Software

While Microsoft Defender Antivirus provides solid baseline protection, some users prefer to use third-party antivirus software for additional features and customization. When choosing third-party antivirus software, consider the following:

1. *Features:* *Different antivirus solutions offer various features such as anti-phishing, firewall, email filtering, and more. Choose one that aligns with your specific needs.*

2. *Performance:* *Some antivirus programs can be resource-intensive and impact system performance. Look for reviews and benchmarks to ensure that the software doesn't slow down your computer.*

3. *Ease of Use:* *User-friendly interfaces and clear settings are essential for managing antivirus software effectively.*

4. *Cost:* *While many antivirus solutions offer free versions, consider whether you need additional premium features and what the associated costs are.*

5. *Independent Testing:* *Check independent antivirus testing organizations' results to see how well a particular antivirus software performs in detecting and blocking threats.*

6. *Updates:* *Ensure that the antivirus software you choose receives regular updates to stay effective against new threats.*

7. *Compatibility:* *Verify that the antivirus software is compatible with Windows 11 and other software you use.*

Remember that you should only run one antivirus program at a time to avoid conflicts and system instability. If you decide to install a third-party antivirus, Windows Defender will typically disable its real-time protection automatically.

In conclusion, Windows Defender in Windows 11 offers solid protection against malware and online threats. However, the choice between using it and a third-party antivirus solution ultimately depends on your specific needs, preferences, and the level of security you require for your computer. Regardless of your choice, regularly updating your antivirus software and staying informed about the latest security threats is crucial for maintaining a secure computing environment.

Section 11.3: Performing System Maintenance and Health Checks

Ensuring the optimal performance and health of your Windows 11 system is crucial to its longevity and efficient operation. In this section, we will discuss various system maintenance tasks and health checks that you should perform regularly to keep your computer running smoothly.

Disk Cleanup and Optimization

Over time, your computer's storage can accumulate unnecessary files and temporary data, which can consume valuable disk space and slow down your system. Windows 11 offers built-in tools for disk cleanup and optimization:

- **Disk Cleanup:** This utility allows you to remove temporary files, system cache, and other unnecessary files from your system. To access it, search for "Disk Cleanup" in the Start menu, select your drive, and let the tool analyze your system for cleanup options.

- **Storage Sense:** Windows 11 includes "Storage Sense," which can automatically free up disk space by removing temporary files and emptying the recycle bin. You can enable and configure Storage Sense in **Settings** > **System** > **Storage**.

- **Optimize Drives:** Regularly optimizing your drives (including SSDs) can help maintain their performance. Search for "Defragment and Optimize Drives" in the Start menu, select your drive, and click "Optimize" to defragment or trim your drives.

Windows Updates

Keeping your Windows 11 system up to date with the latest updates and patches is essential for security and performance. Windows Update automatically downloads and installs updates, but you can also check for updates manually in **Settings** > **Windows Update**.

System Health Checks

Performing regular system health checks can help identify and address potential issues before they become significant problems:

- **Reliability Monitor:** You can access the Reliability Monitor by searching for it in the Start menu. It provides a timeline of system events, errors, and warnings. This information can help diagnose issues and pinpoint their causes.

- **Event Viewer:** The Event Viewer allows you to review detailed logs of system events, errors, and warnings. You can access it by searching for "Event Viewer" in the Start menu. Be cautious when making changes based on event log information, as not all events require action.

- **Windows Memory Diagnostic:** If you suspect issues related to your computer's memory (RAM), you can use the Windows Memory Diagnostic tool. Search for "Windows Memory Diagnostic" in the Start menu, and follow the on-screen instructions to check for memory problems.

Antivirus and Security Scans

Ensure that your antivirus software (whether it's Windows Defender or a third-party solution) is up to date and regularly performs full system scans. Additionally, run periodic malware scans using trusted malware removal tools to detect and remove any threats that might have bypassed your antivirus.

Monitoring the health of your computer's hardware components, such as the CPU, GPU, and hard drive, is essential:

- **Temperature Monitoring:** Use software tools like Core Temp or HWMonitor to monitor the temperature of your CPU and GPU. Overheating can lead to performance issues and hardware damage.

- **SMART Status:** Check the SMART status of your hard drive or SSD using tools like CrystalDiskInfo. SMART status provides information about the health of your storage device.

- **Driver Updates:** Ensure that your hardware drivers are up to date. You can usually download the latest drivers from the manufacturer's website.

Cleaning and Maintenance

Physically clean your computer's components regularly, especially if it's a desktop. Dust and debris can accumulate inside your computer, leading to overheating and performance problems. Ensure proper airflow and ventilation by cleaning fans and components carefully.

Performing these system maintenance and health checks regularly can help you identify and resolve issues proactively, ensuring that your Windows 11 system remains stable, secure, and responsive over time. Regular maintenance can extend the lifespan of your computer and enhance your overall computing experience.

Section 11.4: Understanding User Account Control (UAC) and Permissions

User Account Control (UAC) is a crucial security feature in Windows 11 that helps protect your computer and data by controlling and limiting the permissions of applications and processes. In this section, we'll explore UAC, its purpose, and how to manage it effectively.

What is User Account Control (UAC)?

UAC was introduced in Windows Vista and has been a part of every Windows version since. Its primary purpose is to prevent unauthorized changes to your computer and data by requiring that certain actions and tasks be approved by an administrator or user with administrative privileges.

When UAC is enabled, Windows distinguishes between standard user accounts and administrator accounts. Standard users have limited access to system files and settings, while administrator accounts have elevated privileges. Even if you're using an administrator account, many tasks and applications run with standard user permissions by default.

When an application or process attempts to perform a task that requires elevated privileges (e.g., making system changes, installing software, or modifying critical settings), UAC prompts the user with a dialog box asking for permission. This dialog box is known as the UAC prompt or elevation prompt.

The UAC prompt includes the following options:

- **Yes:** This option allows the task to proceed with administrative privileges. If you initiated the action intentionally, you can click "Yes" to continue.
- **No:** Clicking "No" denies the task the required administrative privileges, and it won't be executed.
- **Show Details:** If available, this option provides more information about the task before making a decision.

Configuring UAC Settings

You can configure UAC settings to meet your security and convenience preferences. To access UAC settings:

1. Open **Control Panel**.
2. Go to **System and Security**.
3. Under **Security and Maintenance**, click on **Change User Account Control settings**.

You'll see a slider with four levels of UAC control:

- **Always notify:** This is the highest security level. It prompts for consent for any action that requires administrative privileges.
- **Notify me only when apps try to make changes:** This is the default setting. It notifies you when apps attempt to make changes but not for Windows settings changes.
- **Notify me only when apps try to make changes (do not dim my desktop):** Similar to the previous setting, but it doesn't dim the screen when showing the UAC prompt.
- **Never notify:** This is the lowest security level. UAC is effectively disabled, and actions requiring administrative privileges proceed without prompts.

It's essential to strike a balance between security and convenience when configuring UAC. While disabling it entirely can make your system more vulnerable to unauthorized changes, setting it too high may lead to frequent prompts, which can be bothersome.

Best Practices with UAC

Here are some best practices for working with UAC:

1. **Keep UAC Enabled:** It's generally recommended to keep UAC enabled to enhance the security of your system.

2. **Use Standard User Accounts:** Whenever possible, use standard user accounts for everyday tasks, reserving administrator accounts for system maintenance and administrative tasks.

3. **Respond Cautiously:** Always be cautious when responding to UAC prompts. Verify the source and purpose of the prompt before clicking "Yes."

4. **Regularly Review UAC Settings:** Periodically review and adjust your UAC settings to find the right balance between security and convenience.

5. **Stay Informed:** Educate yourself about common UAC prompts and the actions they correspond to. This knowledge can help you make informed decisions.

By understanding and effectively managing UAC and permissions in Windows 11, you can maintain a secure and functional computing environment while minimizing the risk of unauthorized changes and potential security threats.

Section 11.5: Creating and Managing System Restore Points

System Restore is a valuable feature in Windows 11 that allows you to revert your computer's system files and settings to a previous state. It can be a lifesaver when your system encounters issues or errors after making significant changes. In this section, we'll explore how to create, manage, and use System Restore points effectively.

What Is a System Restore Point?

A System Restore point is a snapshot of your computer's system files and settings at a specific moment in time. These points serve as backup states that you can revert to when needed. Creating a System Restore point captures the current configuration of your system, including installed applications, device drivers, and system files.

When to Use System Restore

System Restore can be beneficial in several scenarios, including:

1. **Software Installation Issues:** If you experience problems after installing new software or drivers, you can use System Restore to roll back your system to a state before the installation.

2. **Windows Updates Problems:** If a Windows Update causes issues or conflicts with your system, a System Restore point can help you return to a stable configuration.

3. **Malware or Virus Infections:** If your computer becomes infected with malware or viruses, you can use System Restore to go back to a state before the infection occurred.

4. **Configuration Mistakes:** If you accidentally make configuration changes that negatively impact your system's stability, a System Restore point can undo those changes.

Creating a System Restore Point

To create a System Restore point in Windows 11, follow these steps:

1. Open the **Start Menu** and type "Create a restore point." Click on the search result that says "Create a restore point."

2. In the "System Properties" window that opens, go to the "System Restore" tab.

3. Click the "Create" button. You can provide a descriptive name for the restore point to help you identify it later.

4. Click "Create" again to confirm. Windows will now create a restore point, and the process may take a few minutes.

Restoring Your System

To restore your system to a previous state using a System Restore point:

1. Follow the same steps as above to open the "System Properties" window.

2. In the "System Restore" tab, click the "System Restore" button.

3. A wizard will open, guiding you through the restoration process. Select the restore point you want to use and follow the on-screen instructions.

Managing System Restore Points

Windows automatically creates System Restore points when significant changes occur, such as software installations and Windows Updates. However, you can also manually create and manage restore points. Here's how:

1. Open the "System Properties" window as described earlier.

2. In the "System Restore" tab, click the "Configure" button.

3. In the configuration window, you can:

   - Turn off System Restore for specific drives.
   - Adjust the maximum disk space used by System Restore (by default, it uses a percentage of your drive's space).
   - Delete older restore points to free up disk space.

Best Practices for Using System Restore

Here are some best practices for effectively using System Restore in Windows 11:

1. **Regularly Create Restore Points:** Manually create restore points before making significant changes to your system, such as software installations or updates. This ensures you have a known-good state to return to if issues arise.

2. **Keep Enough Disk Space:** Ensure that you have enough free disk space to store System Restore points. If your disk becomes full, Windows may automatically delete older restore points.

3. **Use Other Backup Solutions:** While System Restore is handy, it's not a complete backup solution. Consider using additional backup methods, such as regular data backups or creating system images, for comprehensive data protection.

4. **Verify Your Restore Point:** Before using a restore point, ensure it's from a time when your system was stable and free of issues.

By understanding how to create, manage, and use System Restore points in Windows 11, you can safeguard your system and quickly recover from unexpected problems, ultimately ensuring a smoother and more reliable computing experience.

Chapter 12: Troubleshooting Common Issues

Section 12.1: Diagnosing and Resolving Hardware Issues

In this section, we'll delve into diagnosing and resolving common hardware-related issues that Windows 11 users may encounter. Hardware problems can cause a variety of symptoms, including system crashes, hardware failures, and performance degradation. Identifying and addressing these issues is crucial for maintaining a stable and efficient computing experience.

Identifying Hardware Issues

Hardware problems can manifest in different ways, making it essential to recognize the signs and symptoms. Here are some common indicators of hardware issues:

1. **Blue Screen of Death (BSOD):** Frequent system crashes accompanied by a blue screen error message often point to hardware problems. The error message may contain clues about the specific issue.

2. **Random Freezing or Lockups:** If your computer freezes or locks up unexpectedly, it could be due to hardware issues such as overheating, faulty RAM, or a failing hard drive.

3. **Device Not Recognized:** If a device like a printer, external hard drive, or USB device is not recognized or fails to work correctly, it may be a hardware-related problem.

4. **Slow Performance:** While slow performance can result from various factors, it may be due to hardware limitations or issues. Hardware components like the CPU, RAM, or storage drive can affect system speed.

5. **Unusual Noises:** Unusual noises from your computer, such as clicking, grinding, or buzzing sounds, may indicate problems with hardware components like the hard drive or cooling fans.

Diagnosing Hardware Issues

To diagnose hardware issues, follow these steps:

1. **Check Event Logs:** Windows logs events related to hardware problems. Open the "Event Viewer" and look for error messages or warnings under the "System" and "Hardware Events" categories.

2. **Run Built-in Diagnostics:** Windows offers built-in diagnostic tools that can test various hardware components. For example, you can run the Windows Memory Diagnostic tool to check your RAM's integrity.

3. **Monitor Temperatures:** Overheating can cause hardware issues. Use monitoring software to check the temperature of your CPU and GPU. If they are consistently running too hot, it may indicate a cooling problem.

4. **Inspect Physical Connections:** Ensure that all hardware components are securely connected. Loose cables or connectors can lead to malfunctions.

5. **Test External Devices:** If you suspect an external device is causing problems, try connecting it to another computer to see if the issue persists.

Common Hardware Issues and Solutions

Let's explore some common hardware problems and their solutions:

1. Faulty RAM:
- **Issue:** Frequent BSODs, system crashes, or application errors.
- **Solution:** Replace or reseat the RAM modules. Use the Windows Memory Diagnostic tool to identify issues.

2. Overheating:
- **Issue:** System instability, random freezes, or unexpected shutdowns.
- **Solution:** Clean dust from fans and heatsinks, ensure proper airflow, and consider using a cooling pad for laptops.

3. Hard Drive Failure:
- **Issue:** Clicking or grinding noises, slow performance, or file errors.
- **Solution:** Back up your data immediately, as hard drive failure can result in data loss. Replace the failing drive with a new one.

4. Graphics Card Problems:
- **Issue:** Display artifacts, graphical glitches, or system crashes during graphics-intensive tasks.
- **Solution:** Update graphics card drivers and ensure proper ventilation and power supply for the GPU.

5. USB Device Issues:
- **Issue:** USB devices not recognized or not working correctly.
- **Solution:** Try connecting the device to different USB ports, updating USB drivers, or testing the device on another computer.

6. Network Adapter Problems:
- **Issue:** Network connectivity issues, frequent disconnections.
- **Solution:** Update network adapter drivers, check for physical damage to cables, or replace the network adapter if necessary.

While many hardware issues can be diagnosed and resolved by users, some may require professional assistance, especially if they involve intricate components like the motherboard or require specialized tools. If you are unsure about how to proceed or suspect a severe hardware problem, consider seeking help from a qualified technician or contacting your device's manufacturer for warranty support.

By understanding common hardware issues, their symptoms, and diagnostic procedures, you can effectively troubleshoot and resolve hardware-related problems, ensuring the longevity and reliability of your Windows 11 computer.

Section 12.2: Troubleshooting Software and Application Errors

In this section, we will explore the process of troubleshooting common software and application errors on a Windows 11 system. Software-related issues can range from application crashes and compatibility problems to system instability caused by software conflicts. Addressing these issues effectively is crucial for maintaining a smooth and productive computing experience.

Identifying Software and Application Errors

Before diving into troubleshooting, it's essential to recognize the signs of software and application errors. Here are some common indicators:

1. **Application Crashes:** When a specific program consistently crashes or freezes, it indicates a software issue. Windows may display error messages or simply close the application.

2. **Slow or Unresponsive System:** Sluggish system performance, delays in application startup, or overall system unresponsiveness can result from software problems.

3. **Compatibility Errors:** Some applications may not work correctly on Windows 11 due to compatibility issues. This can manifest as error messages, missing features, or unexpected behavior.

4. **Error Messages:** Windows often provides error messages that offer clues about the nature of the problem. These messages can be helpful in diagnosing the issue.

Troubleshooting Software and Application Errors

To address software and application errors effectively, follow these steps:

1. **Check for Updates:** Ensure that both Windows 11 and your installed applications are up to date. Developers frequently release updates to address bugs and improve compatibility.

2. **Restart Your Computer:** Sometimes, a simple restart can resolve software glitches and temporary issues.

3. **Use Safe Mode:** Booting Windows in Safe Mode loads a minimal set of drivers and may help identify if a third-party application is causing the problem. If the issue doesn't occur in Safe Mode, it likely relates to third-party software.

4. **Review Error Messages:** Pay attention to any error messages or codes displayed. Searching for these online or in Microsoft's official support documentation can often provide solutions.

5. **Check for Conflicting Software:** Sometimes, multiple applications or background processes can conflict with each other. Identify any recent software installations or updates that coincide with the appearance of the issue.

6. **Update or Reinstall Problematic Applications:** If a specific application is causing trouble, update it to the latest version. If the problem persists, consider reinstalling the application.

Common Software and Application Issues and Solutions

Let's explore some common software and application problems and their solutions:

1. Application Crashes:
- **Issue:** An application crashes immediately upon startup or during use.
- **Solution:** Update the application to the latest version, check for system requirements, and ensure your device meets them. If the issue continues, contact the application's support team for assistance.

2. Compatibility Problems:
- **Issue:** An application designed for older Windows versions doesn't work correctly on Windows 11.
- **Solution:** Check the application's official website for updates or patches specifically designed for Windows 11. If none are available, consider using compatibility mode or seeking alternatives.

3. Slow System Performance:
- **Issue:** The system is sluggish, and applications respond slowly.
- **Solution:** Close unnecessary background applications, ensure your system meets the application's system requirements, and consider upgrading hardware components like RAM or storage if necessary.

4. Missing or Corrupt Files:
- **Issue:** Application or system files are missing or corrupted, leading to errors or crashes.

- **Solution:** Use the built-in Windows "System File Checker" tool (sfc /scannow) to scan and repair corrupted system files. For applications, consider reinstalling them to replace missing or damaged files.

5. *Software Conflicts:*
- **Issue:** Multiple applications or background processes conflict with each other.
- **Solution:** Identify conflicting software through trial and error or by reviewing system logs. Uninstall or disable conflicting applications or seek guidance from their support resources.

Seeking Additional Help

While these troubleshooting steps can resolve many software and application issues, some problems may be more complex or require specialized knowledge. If you encounter persistent issues that you cannot resolve on your own, consider seeking assistance from the application's support team or a professional IT service provider. Additionally, you can explore online forums and communities where experts and users share solutions to various software-related problems.

By understanding how to identify and address software and application errors, you can enhance the stability and functionality of your Windows 11 system, ensuring a smoother and more productive computing experience.

Section 12.3: Network Troubleshooting and Internet Connectivity Problems

In this section, we will delve into network troubleshooting and common internet connectivity problems that Windows 11 users may encounter. A stable and reliable internet connection is essential for various tasks, from browsing the web and streaming content to online gaming and remote work. When issues arise, it's crucial to diagnose and resolve them efficiently to minimize disruption.

Identifying Internet Connectivity Issues

Before proceeding with troubleshooting, it's essential to determine whether you are experiencing internet connectivity issues. Here are some common signs:

1. **No Internet Access:** You are unable to connect to any websites, services, or online applications, and Windows reports no internet access.

2. **Slow Internet:** Your internet connection is exceptionally slow, resulting in delays when loading web pages or streaming content.

3. **Intermittent Connection:** Your connection frequently drops or experiences periodic disruptions, making online activities frustrating.

4. **Limited Connectivity:** Windows reports limited connectivity or displays an error message when trying to connect to a network.

To diagnose and resolve internet connectivity problems on Windows 11, follow these steps:

1. **Check Network Cables and Hardware:** If you are using a wired connection, ensure that Ethernet cables are securely plugged in and that your router or modem is functioning correctly. For wireless connections, check that Wi-Fi routers and access points are operational.

2. **Restart Your Router and Modem:** Power cycle your router and modem by unplugging them from the power source, waiting for a few seconds, and then plugging them back in. This can often resolve temporary connectivity issues.

3. **Verify Network Status:** Check if other devices on the same network are experiencing similar issues. If all devices are affected, the problem may be with your internet service provider (ISP).

4. **Run Windows Network Troubleshooter:** Windows includes a built-in Network Troubleshooter that can identify and attempt to fix common connectivity problems. To run it, right-click the network icon in the taskbar and select "Troubleshoot problems."

5. **Update Network Drivers:** Outdated or incompatible network drivers can cause connectivity problems. Ensure that your network adapter drivers are up to date by visiting the manufacturer's website or using Windows Update.

6. **Check Firewall and Security Software:** Overly restrictive firewall settings or security software can sometimes block internet access. Temporarily disable these software components to see if they are the cause of the problem.

7. **Reset Network Settings:** Windows provides an option to reset network settings to their defaults. This can resolve configuration issues. To do this, go to Settings > Network & Internet > Status, and under "Network reset," click "Reset now."

8. **Review IP Configuration:** Check your IP configuration by opening the Command Prompt and running the command `ipconfig /all`. Ensure that your IP address, subnet mask, default gateway, and DNS servers are correctly configured.

9. **Flush DNS Cache:** DNS issues can cause connectivity problems. You can flush the DNS cache by opening the Command Prompt and running `ipconfig /flushdns`.

10. **Test DNS Resolution:** Use the `nslookup` command in the Command Prompt to test DNS resolution. For example, you can run `nslookup google.com` to check if your system can resolve domain names.

Let's explore some specific internet connectivity issues and their potential solutions:

1. Wi-Fi Connection Drops:

- **Issue:** Your Wi-Fi connection frequently drops or disconnects.
- **Solution:** Ensure that your router firmware is up to date. Try changing the Wi-Fi channel to reduce interference, and ensure that your device is within a reasonable range of the router.

2. **No Internet Access:

- **Issue:** Windows reports no internet access even though you are connected to a network.
- **Solution:** Check if there is a captive portal or login page that requires authentication on the network. Verify that your network settings, including IP configuration and DNS, are correct.

3. **Slow Internet Speed:

- **Issue:** Your internet connection is slower than expected.
- **Solution:** Contact your ISP to confirm your plan's speed. Check for background downloads or uploads that may be consuming bandwidth. Consider upgrading your plan if necessary.

4. **Limited Connectivity:

- **Issue:** Windows reports limited connectivity when connecting to a network.
- **Solution:** Restart your router and modem, update network drivers, and check for IP conflicts or incorrect network settings.

5. **Intermittent Connection:

- **Issue:** Your connection drops intermittently.
- **Solution:** Check for nearby electronic devices or appliances that may interfere with Wi-Fi signals. Position your router away from potential sources of interference.

Seeking Further Assistance

If you have followed these troubleshooting steps and continue to experience internet connectivity issues, it may be necessary to contact your ISP for assistance. They can perform diagnostics on their end and send a technician if required. Additionally, you can consult Windows support resources or online forums for specific guidance on your particular issue.

By effectively troubleshooting and addressing internet connectivity

Section 12.4: Resolving Display and Graphics Issues

In this section, we will focus on troubleshooting and resolving common display and graphics issues that Windows 11 users may encounter. Problems related to display and graphics can manifest in various ways, including screen artifacts, flickering, resolution problems, and driver conflicts. Resolving these issues is essential to ensure a smooth and visually appealing computing experience.

Identifying Display and Graphics Issues

Before we delve into troubleshooting, it's crucial to identify the specific display or graphics problem you are facing. Here are some common signs of display and graphics issues:

1. **Screen Flickering:** The screen intermittently flickers or flashes.

2. **Resolution Problems:** The display resolution is incorrect, resulting in a blurry or stretched screen.

3. **Artifacting:** Unusual visual artifacts, such as random lines or distortions, appear on the screen.

4. **Driver Errors:** Windows reports errors related to display drivers, such as "Display driver stopped responding and has recovered."

5. **No Signal:** The monitor displays a "No Signal" message even when the computer is powered on.

Troubleshooting Display and Graphics Issues

To address display and graphics problems in Windows 11, follow these troubleshooting steps:

1. **Check Physical Connections:** Ensure that all cables connecting your monitor or display device to the computer are securely plugged in. Loose connections can lead to display problems.

2. **Update Graphics Drivers:** Outdated or incompatible graphics drivers are a common cause of display issues. Visit the website of your graphics card manufacturer (e.g., NVIDIA, AMD, Intel) to download and install the latest drivers.

3. **Adjust Display Resolution:** Right-click on the desktop and select "Display settings." Verify that the display resolution is set to the recommended value for your monitor. Adjust it if necessary.

4. **Roll Back Graphics Driver:** If you recently updated your graphics driver and encountered issues, consider rolling back to a previous driver version. To do this, go to Device Manager, locate your graphics card, right-click, and select "Properties." Under the "Driver" tab, click "Roll Back Driver" if the option is available.

5. **Check for Driver Conflicts:** In some cases, conflicts between different drivers can lead to graphics issues. Make sure that your display, graphics, and chipset drivers are all up to date.

6. **Disable Hardware Acceleration:** Some applications, especially web browsers, use hardware acceleration for rendering. Disabling hardware acceleration in application settings can sometimes resolve graphics problems.

7. **Update Windows:** Ensure that Windows 11 is up to date with the latest updates and patches. Microsoft frequently releases updates that address known graphics-related issues.

8. **Test in Safe Mode:** Boot your computer into Safe Mode (press F8 or Shift + F8 during startup) to check if the issue persists. If it doesn't, it may indicate that a third-party application or driver is causing the problem.

9. **Run Windows Memory Diagnostic:** Graphics issues can sometimes be related to faulty RAM. Run the Windows Memory Diagnostic tool to check for memory problems. To do this, search for "Windows Memory Diagnostic" in the Start menu and follow the instructions.

10. **Check for Overheating:** Overheating can cause graphics problems. Ensure that your computer is adequately cooled, and clean any dust from cooling fans and vents.

11. **Scan for Malware:** Malware infections can lead to various system issues, including graphics problems. Perform a full system scan using Windows Defender or a reputable antivirus program.

Specific Graphics-Related Problems and Solutions

Let's explore some specific graphics-related problems and their potential solutions:

1. Screen Tearing:
- **Issue:** Screen tearing occurs when frames rendered by the GPU don't align correctly with the monitor's refresh rate, resulting in horizontal tearing.
- **Solution:** Enable V-Sync (Vertical Synchronization) in graphics settings to synchronize frame rendering with the monitor's refresh rate.

2. Artifacting and Visual Glitches:
- **Issue:** Visual artifacts or glitches appear on the screen.
- **Solution:** Check for overheating, update graphics drivers, and test the graphics card in another system to rule out hardware issues.

3. Multiple Displays Not Detected:
- **Issue:** Windows doesn't detect additional monitors.
- **Solution:** Check cable connections, update graphics drivers, and use the "Detect" button in the Display settings to identify additional displays.

4. Resolution Mismatch:

- **Issue:** The display resolution doesn't match the monitor's native resolution.
- **Solution:** Adjust the resolution in Display settings to match your monitor's recommended resolution.

5. No Signal on Monitor:

- **Issue:** The monitor displays a "No Signal" message.
- **Solution:** Ensure the cable connections are secure, check the monitor's input source, and verify that the graphics card is properly seated in its slot.

6. Graphics Driver Crashes:

- **Issue:** Windows reports that the graphics driver has crashed.
- **Solution:** Update or roll back the graphics driver, ensure proper cooling, and check for overclocking issues if applicable.

Seeking Further Assistance

If you have followed these troubleshooting steps and continue to experience display and graphics issues, it may be necessary to contact your graphics card manufacturer's support or seek assistance from a professional technician. Complex hardware-related problems may require in-depth diagnosis and potential hardware replacement to resolve.

By systematically addressing and resolving display and graphics issues, you can ensure a smoother and more visually appealing computing experience on Windows 11.

Section 12.5: Advanced Troubleshooting Techniques and Tools

In this section, we will explore advanced troubleshooting techniques and tools for addressing complex and persistent issues on your Windows 11 computer. While earlier sections covered common problems and their solutions, advanced troubleshooting is necessary when you encounter stubborn or less common issues that require a deeper understanding of Windows internals.

Event Viewer and Logs

Event Viewer is a built-in Windows tool that logs various system events, errors, and warnings. It can provide valuable information about what's happening behind the scenes on your system. Here's how to use it:

1. Press Win + X and select "Event Viewer" from the context menu.
2. In the Event Viewer, navigate through the different logs such as "Windows Logs" and "Applications and Services Logs" to find relevant error messages or warnings.
3. Clicking on an event will provide details, including event descriptions and error codes. This information can be useful for diagnosing specific problems.

System File Checker (SFC)

The **System File Checker (SFC)** is a command-line tool that scans and repairs corrupted or missing system files. It can be helpful when you suspect that system files are causing issues. Here's how to use it:

1. Open a Command Prompt with administrative privileges by searching for "cmd" or "Command Prompt" in the Start menu, right-clicking it, and selecting "Run as administrator."

2. In the Command Prompt, type the following command and press Enter:

    `sfc /scannow`

3. The tool will scan and attempt to repair any corrupted system files. Follow the on-screen instructions if prompted.

DISM (Deployment Imaging Service and Management Tool)

The **DISM** tool is another command-line utility that can be used to repair Windows images and system files. It's particularly useful when the SFC tool doesn't fully resolve the issue. Here's how to use it:

1. Open a Command Prompt with administrative privileges as mentioned earlier.

2. In the Command Prompt, type the following command and press Enter:

    `DISM /Online /Cleanup-Image /RestoreHealth`

3. Allow the tool to complete the scan and repair process. This may take some time.

Windows Repair and Reset Options

Windows 11 provides several repair and reset options that can help you resolve persistent issues:

1. **Reset This PC:** This feature allows you to reinstall Windows 11 while keeping your personal files intact. It can be accessed in **Settings > System > Recovery > Reset this PC**.

2. **System Restore:** If you have previously created system restore points, you can use them to revert your system to a previous state where it was functioning correctly. Search for "Create a restore point" in the Start menu to access this feature.

3. **Windows Recovery Environment (WinRE):** You can access WinRE by holding down the Shift key while clicking the "Restart" option from the Start menu. This environment provides various troubleshooting and recovery tools.

Driver Verifier is a Windows tool that monitors drivers for potential issues that could cause system crashes. While it's a powerful tool, it should be used with caution as it can make your system unstable if misused. Here's how to enable it:

1. Open a Command Prompt with administrative privileges.

2. Type the following command and press Enter to start Driver Verifier:

   ```
   verifier
   ```

3. Follow the on-screen instructions to configure and enable the verifier. You can choose to check all drivers or select specific ones.

Professional Assistance

If you've exhausted all the troubleshooting steps and still face unresolved issues, it may be time to seek professional assistance. Certified technicians and IT specialists have the expertise and tools to diagnose and resolve complex problems. Consider reaching out to your computer manufacturer's support or a local IT service provider for assistance.

Remember to back up your important data before attempting any advanced troubleshooting or system repairs to avoid data loss.

In conclusion, advanced troubleshooting techniques and tools are valuable resources when dealing with complex and stubborn issues on your Windows 11 system. Event Viewer, SFC, DISM, Windows repair options, and Driver Verifier can help diagnose and resolve a wide range of problems. However, if you're unsure about using these tools or your issue persists, don't hesitate to seek professional assistance.

Chapter 13: Enhancing Accessibility

Section 13.1: Exploring Accessibility Features in Windows 11

Windows 11 places a strong emphasis on accessibility, striving to make the operating system as inclusive as possible for users with diverse needs. In this section, we will explore the accessibility features and tools built into Windows 11, highlighting how they can benefit individuals with disabilities and improve the overall user experience.

1. Accessibility Center

Windows 11 introduces the Accessibility Center, a central hub for managing and customizing accessibility settings. To access it, go to **Settings > Accessibility**. Here, you'll find a range of options to tailor the user interface, display, audio, and input settings to your specific requirements.

2. Ease of Access Settings

Within the Accessibility Center, you'll discover the Ease of Access settings. These settings encompass a wide variety of options to enhance the user experience:

- **Display:** Adjust text size, contrast, and color filters to make content more readable.
- **Hearing:** Configure sound enhancements, closed captions, and audio alerts.
- **Interaction:** Customize mouse, keyboard, and touchpad settings for easier navigation.
- **Voice Typing:** Utilize speech recognition for hands-free text input.

3. Magnifier

The Magnifier tool in Windows 11 enables users to zoom in on parts of the screen, making content more visible. You can activate Magnifier by pressing Win + + (plus key) and control it with various keyboard shortcuts. It's particularly useful for users with visual impairments or those who need to examine fine details.

4. Narrator

Narrator is a built-in screen reader that provides spoken feedback for users with visual impairments. To activate Narrator, press Ctrl + Win + Enter. It reads aloud on-screen content, making it accessible to users who rely on audio feedback.

5. Speech Recognition

Windows 11 includes a powerful speech recognition feature that allows users to control their computer and input text using voice commands. By saying "Open [app name]" or "Type [text]," users can interact with their computer hands-free. This feature benefits individuals with mobility or dexterity limitations.

6. On-Screen Keyboard

The On-Screen Keyboard in Windows 11 provides an alternative input method for users who cannot use a physical keyboard. You can access it from the Accessibility Center or by pressing Ctrl + Win + O. It includes word prediction and various customization options.

7. Other Accessibility Features

Windows 11 also offers a range of other accessibility features, including:

- **High Contrast Mode:** Enhances readability by increasing the contrast between text and background.
- **Sticky Keys:** Allows users to perform keyboard shortcuts one key at a time.
- **Filter Keys:** Ignores brief or repeated keystrokes, reducing input errors.
- **Mouse Pointer Enhancements:** Makes the mouse pointer easier to see and locate.

8. Third-Party Accessibility Apps

In addition to the built-in accessibility features, Windows 11 supports third-party accessibility apps and devices. These can further enhance the user experience by addressing specific needs or preferences. Many hardware and software developers create products and applications designed to work seamlessly with Windows 11's accessibility framework.

9. Inclusive Design

Windows 11's commitment to accessibility extends to the development of apps and software by third-party developers. Microsoft provides resources and guidelines for creating inclusive software that can be used by all individuals, regardless of their abilities. Developers are encouraged to embrace inclusive design principles to ensure that their applications are accessible to the widest possible audience.

10. Conclusion

Accessibility is a fundamental aspect of Windows 11, reflecting Microsoft's dedication to creating an operating system that is welcoming and functional for everyone. Whether you have specific accessibility needs or want to improve the overall usability of your computer, Windows 11's accessibility features offer a wealth of options to explore and customize, making the digital world more accessible and inclusive.

Section 13.2: Customizing Visual, Audio, and Input Settings for Accessibility

In Windows 11, accessibility features extend beyond just providing alternative input methods or screen readers. Users can customize various visual, audio, and input settings to create a personalized and more accessible computing environment. This section explores these customization options and how they can benefit individuals with diverse needs.

Visual Customization

1. High Contrast Mode

High Contrast Mode is a visual setting that enhances readability by increasing the contrast between text and background colors. It can be beneficial for users with visual impairments or those who find standard themes hard to read. To enable High Contrast Mode, go to **Settings > Accessibility > Display > High contrast**.

2. Customizing Text Size and Fonts

Windows 11 allows users to adjust text size and fonts to make content more readable. You can increase or decrease text size and choose from a variety of fonts to suit your preferences. These settings are available in **Settings > Accessibility > Display > Text size and fonts**.

3. Cursor and Pointer Customization

For users who have trouble locating the mouse cursor, Windows 11 offers cursor customization options. You can change the size and color of the cursor, making it more visible on the screen. To access these settings, go to **Settings > Accessibility > Mouse pointer**.

Audio Customization

1. Sound Enhancements

Windows 11 provides sound enhancements that can improve audio clarity for users with hearing impairments. These enhancements include options to boost bass, adjust treble, and fine-tune audio settings. You can find these settings in **Settings > Accessibility > Hearing > Sound enhancements**.

2. Closed Captions

Closed captions are a vital accessibility feature for users who are deaf or hard of hearing. Windows 11 offers built-in closed caption settings that can be customized to display captions for various types of content. You can configure closed captions in **Settings > Accessibility > Hearing > Closed captions**.

3. Visual Alerts

Visual alerts are notifications that accompany sounds to provide visual cues for system events. These can be particularly helpful for individuals who are deaf or hard of hearing. You can enable visual alerts in **Settings > Accessibility > Hearing > Visual alerts**.

Input Customization

1. Keyboard and Mouse Settings

Customizing keyboard and mouse settings can make interaction with the computer more comfortable. Windows 11 allows you to adjust the keyboard repeat rate, set keyboard shortcuts, and customize mouse behavior. These settings are available in **Settings > Accessibility > Interaction**.

2. Sticky Keys

Sticky Keys is an accessibility feature that makes it easier to perform keyboard shortcuts for users with mobility or dexterity limitations. When enabled, Sticky Keys allows you to press one key at a time for keyboard shortcuts instead of multiple keys simultaneously. To turn on Sticky Keys, go to **Settings > Accessibility > Interaction > Sticky Keys**.

3. Mouse Pointer Enhancements

Windows 11 offers settings to enhance the mouse pointer's visibility. You can change the pointer's size, color, and behavior, making it easier to locate and follow. These settings are accessible in **Settings > Accessibility > Mouse pointer**.

Conclusion

Windows 11's customizable visual, audio, and input settings provide users with a powerful toolkit for tailoring their computing experience to their specific needs. Whether you require high-contrast visuals, closed captions, or customized keyboard shortcuts, Windows 11 offers a wide range of accessibility features that can enhance your overall usability and accessibility. These options empower individuals with disabilities to use their computers more effectively and independently, fostering a more inclusive digital environment.

Section 13.3: Using Narrator, Magnifier, and Speech Recognition

Windows 11 includes built-in assistive technologies that cater to individuals with varying accessibility needs. This section focuses on three essential accessibility features: Narrator, Magnifier, and Speech Recognition, each designed to enhance the user experience for specific groups of users.

Narrator: A Screen Reader for the Visually Impaired

Narrator is a screen-reading tool that reads aloud text, buttons, and other elements on the screen for users with visual impairments. It is especially valuable for individuals who rely on auditory cues to navigate and interact with their computers.

To enable Narrator, press Ctrl + Win + Enter. This keyboard shortcut toggles Narrator on and off. Once activated, Narrator provides spoken feedback about what's happening on the screen. Users can customize Narrator settings by going to **Settings > Accessibility > Narrator**.

Key Narrator features and settings include:

- **Voice Options**: Users can choose from various voices and adjust the voice rate, pitch, and volume to suit their preferences.

- **Narrator Commands**: Windows 11 provides a list of keyboard shortcuts and voice commands to control Narrator's behavior effectively.

- **Braille Support**: Narrator offers Braille display compatibility, allowing users to read Braille output alongside the spoken text.

- **Customization**: Users can customize the verbosity, punctuation, and other aspects of how Narrator provides feedback.

Magnifier: Enlarging On-Screen Content

Magnifier is an essential tool for individuals with low vision or visual impairments. It allows users to zoom in on specific parts of the screen, making text and images more readable.

To activate Magnifier, press Ctrl + Win + + to zoom in, and Ctrl + Win + - to zoom out. Users can also launch Magnifier from **Settings > Accessibility > Magnifier**.

Key Magnifier features and settings include:

- **Zoom Levels**: Users can adjust the level of magnification to suit their needs. Windows 11 provides various zoom options, including full-screen magnification or a focused lens.

- **Color Filters**: Magnifier allows users to apply color filters to enhance visibility. This can help individuals with color blindness or specific visual impairments.

- **Follow Mouse Cursor**: Users can choose whether the magnified view follows the mouse cursor or remains fixed in one place.

- **Keyboard Shortcuts**: Windows 11 offers keyboard shortcuts for controlling Magnifier zoom levels and other settings.

Speech Recognition: Hands-Free Computer Interaction

Speech Recognition is a powerful accessibility feature that enables hands-free interaction with Windows 11. It is particularly valuable for individuals with mobility impairments who may have difficulty using traditional input devices.

To set up Speech Recognition, go to **Settings > Accessibility > Speech recognition** and follow the setup wizard. Once configured, users can control their computer, dictate text, open applications, and execute commands using voice input.

Key Speech Recognition features and settings include:

- **Voice Training**: Windows 11 allows users to train the system to recognize their voice accurately, improving accuracy and responsiveness.

- **Voice Commands**: Users can perform a wide range of actions using voice commands, such as opening specific applications, navigating menus, and composing text.

- **Custom Commands**: Advanced users can create custom voice commands for executing personalized actions or automating tasks.

- **Voice Feedback**: Speech Recognition provides voice feedback to confirm that it has recognized and executed the user's commands.

In summary, Windows 11's accessibility features, including Narrator, Magnifier, and Speech Recognition, empower individuals with disabilities to use their computers effectively. These tools cater to users with visual impairments, low vision, and mobility limitations, enhancing their overall computing experience and promoting digital inclusion.

Section 13.4: Accessibility Tips for Applications and Browsers

Ensuring that applications and web browsers are accessible to all users, including those with disabilities, is a critical aspect of software development and website design. In this section, we'll discuss essential accessibility tips for developers, designers, and content creators to make their digital products more inclusive.

1. Use Semantic HTML

When developing web content, use semantic HTML elements (e.g., <nav>, <header>, <button>, <table>) to provide structure and meaning to your content. These elements convey information to assistive technologies and make it easier for users with disabilities to navigate and understand your content.

For example, use proper heading elements (<h1> to <h6>) to create a logical heading structure. Screen readers use this hierarchy to provide context and facilitate navigation.

2. Provide Alternative Text for Images

Images and graphics should always include descriptive alternative text (alt text). Alt text serves as a textual equivalent of the image and is essential for users with visual impairments who rely on screen readers. Ensure that alt text is concise and conveys the image's purpose or content.

```
<img src="example.jpg" alt="A red apple on a wooden table">
```

3. Create Keyboard-Friendly Interfaces

Ensure that all interactive elements, such as buttons, links, and form fields, can be easily navigated and activated using a keyboard. Users with mobility impairments often rely on keyboard navigation or assistive technologies like speech recognition.

Use the `tabindex` attribute to specify the order in which elements receive focus when navigating with the Tab key. Avoid using elements that cannot be accessed or activated via keyboard input.

4. Test with Screen Readers

Regularly test your applications and websites with popular screen readers like NVDA (NonVisual Desktop Access), JAWS, or VoiceOver (for macOS/iOS). This helps you identify accessibility issues and ensure that your content is properly interpreted by assistive technologies.

5. Maintain Proper Contrast

Text should have sufficient contrast against its background to be easily readable. Check color contrast ratios and adhere to the Web Content Accessibility Guidelines (WCAG) standards. There are online tools and browser extensions available to assist in evaluating color contrast.

6. Offer Text Transcripts and Captions

For multimedia content like videos and podcasts, provide text transcripts and captions. Transcripts allow users with hearing impairments to access audio content, while captions benefit users who are deaf or hard of hearing.

7. Implement ARIA Roles and Attributes

ARIA (Accessible Rich Internet Applications) roles and attributes can enhance the accessibility of dynamic web content and single-page applications. Use ARIA roles like `role="button"`, `role="menu"`, or `role="dialog"` to convey the purpose and behavior of interface components to assistive technologies.

8. Focus on Keyboard Accessibility in Forms

Forms should be keyboard accessible, with clear and logical tab orders. Use `<label>` elements associated with form controls to provide context, and ensure that form validation errors are clearly communicated to all users, including those using screen readers.

9. Test for Responsive Design

Ensure that your website or application is responsive and works well on various devices and screen sizes. Users with disabilities may rely on different assistive technologies and may use a range of devices to access your content.

10. Keep Content Simple and Consistent

Clear and concise content benefits all users, but it is especially important for those with cognitive disabilities. Maintain consistent navigation menus and layouts, and avoid excessive use of jargon or complex language.

By following these accessibility tips, developers and content creators can contribute to a more inclusive digital environment. Accessibility is not only a legal requirement in many regions but also a moral and ethical imperative to ensure equal access to information and services for all users.

Section 13.5: Creating an Inclusive Computing Environment

Creating an inclusive computing environment goes beyond adhering to accessibility guidelines; it's about fostering a culture of diversity and ensuring that everyone, regardless of their abilities, feels welcome and empowered in the digital world. In this final section, we'll explore strategies to create a more inclusive computing environment.

1. Raise Awareness

Start by raising awareness among your team members, colleagues, and stakeholders about the importance of digital inclusion. Educate them about the challenges faced by people with disabilities and the benefits of creating accessible content and products.

2. Train and Empower

Provide training and resources to your development and design teams on accessibility best practices. Equip them with the knowledge and tools to create inclusive digital experiences. Encourage team members to attend workshops and webinars on accessibility topics.

3. Involve Users with Disabilities

Include users with disabilities in the design and testing phases of your projects. Their feedback and insights are invaluable for identifying and addressing accessibility issues. Conduct usability tests with assistive technologies to gather real-world feedback.

4. Prioritize Accessibility

Make accessibility a top priority throughout your project lifecycle. Allocate time and resources for accessibility testing, audits, and improvements. Integrate accessibility into your design and development processes rather than treating it as an afterthought.

5. Embrace Universal Design

Universal design principles promote the creation of products and content that are usable by the widest possible audience. Strive for simplicity, clarity, and flexibility in your designs, ensuring that they accommodate diverse needs and preferences.

6. Leverage Inclusive Language

Use inclusive language in your documentation, user interfaces, and communication materials. Avoid terms that might be offensive or exclusionary. Consider providing options for users to customize the interface's language and tone.

7. Foster Collaboration

Encourage cross-functional collaboration between designers, developers, content creators, and accessibility experts. Regular communication and collaboration can lead to more effective solutions and a shared commitment to accessibility.

8. Stay Informed

Stay up-to-date with the latest developments in accessibility standards and guidelines. Accessibility is an evolving field, and new technologies and best practices continue to emerge. Subscribe to relevant newsletters, follow accessibility advocates, and participate in industry discussions.

9. Celebrate Diversity

Recognize and celebrate the diversity of your users. Showcase stories and testimonials from individuals with disabilities who have benefited from your accessible products or content. Highlight the positive impact of your inclusive efforts.

10. Seek Feedback

Invite feedback from your users, especially those with disabilities. Provide multiple channels for feedback, such as email, surveys, and user forums. Act on feedback promptly and demonstrate your commitment to continuous improvement.

11. Advocate for Accessibility

Advocate for accessibility within your organization and industry. Share success stories, case studies, and the business benefits of accessibility. Encourage others to adopt inclusive practices and contribute to a more accessible digital landscape.

12. Lead by Example

Demonstrate leadership in creating an inclusive computing environment. Implement accessible practices in your own work and inspire others to follow suit. Be a role model for accessibility and inclusivity.

In conclusion, creating an inclusive computing environment requires a combination of technical knowledge, cultural change, and a deep commitment to ensuring equal access and participation for all. By following these strategies and fostering a culture of inclusivity, you can contribute to a more accessible and equitable digital world. Accessibility is not just a checkbox; it's a journey that should be integrated into the core values of your organization and embraced by all members of your team.

Chapter 14: Virtualization and Managing Multiple Environments

Virtualization technology has become an integral part of modern computing, enabling users to run multiple operating systems and environments on a single physical machine. In this chapter, we'll explore the concept of virtualization in Windows 11 and how to manage multiple environments efficiently.

Section 14.1: Introduction to Virtualization in Windows 11

Virtualization is the process of creating a virtual or software-based representation of physical hardware, allowing you to run multiple operating systems (guests) simultaneously on a single physical machine (host). Windows 11 provides robust virtualization capabilities through features like Hyper-V and Windows Subsystem for Linux (WSL).

Understanding Hyper-V

Hyper-V is a hypervisor-based virtualization platform developed by Microsoft. It allows you to create and manage virtual machines (VMs) running various guest operating systems, including Windows, Linux, and others. Hyper-V is available on Windows 11 Pro, Enterprise, and Education editions.

Enabling Hyper-V

To enable Hyper-V on your Windows 11 machine, follow these steps:

1. Open "Control Panel" from the Start menu.

2. Click on "Programs."

3. Select "Programs and Features."

4. Click on "Turn Windows features on or off" on the left panel.

5. Check the box next to "Hyper-V" and click "OK."

6. Restart your computer to apply the changes.

Introducing Windows Subsystem for Linux (WSL)

WSL is a compatibility layer for running a Linux kernel and user-mode utilities directly within Windows. It allows developers and users to work with Linux distributions seamlessly alongside their Windows environment. WSL 2, available in Windows 11, offers significant performance improvements over its predecessor.

Installing WSL

To install WSL on Windows 11, follow these steps:

1. Open PowerShell as an administrator.

2. Run the following command to enable the Virtual Machine Platform feature:

```
dism.exe /online /enable-feature /featurename:VirtualMachinePlatform /a
ll /norestart
```

3. Install the WSL 2 Linux kernel update package from the Microsoft Kernel GitHub page.

4. Set WSL 2 as the default version:

```
wsl --set-default-version 2
```

5. Install a Linux distribution of your choice from the Microsoft Store or using the wsl --install command.

With Hyper-V and WSL, you can create isolated environments for development, testing, and running applications without affecting your primary Windows installation. These virtualization technologies open up a world of possibilities for managing multiple environments efficiently on your Windows 11 system. In the following sections, we'll delve deeper into managing virtual machines with Hyper-V and working with Linux distributions using WSL.

Section 14.2: Setting Up and Using Windows Subsystem for Linux (WSL)

Windows Subsystem for Linux (WSL) is a feature in Windows 11 that allows you to run a Linux distribution alongside your Windows environment. It provides a seamless way for developers and users to work with Linux tools, utilities, and even graphical applications on their Windows machine. In this section, we'll explore how to set up and use WSL effectively.

Installing WSL

Before using WSL, you need to install it on your Windows 11 system. Here are the steps to get started:

1. **Open PowerShell as an Administrator:** To do this, search for "PowerShell" in the Start menu, right-click on it, and choose "Run as administrator."

2. **Enable the Virtual Machine Platform feature:** Run the following command to enable the necessary feature:

```
dism.exe /online /enable-feature /featurename:VirtualMachinePlatform /a
ll /norestart
```

This step prepares your system for running WSL 2.

3. **Install the WSL 2 Linux kernel update package:** You can download it from the Microsoft Kernel GitHub page. Once downloaded, double-click the package to install it.

4. **Set WSL 2 as the default version:** Run the following command in PowerShell:

```
wsl --set-default-version 2
```

This ensures that any new Linux distributions you install will use WSL 2.

5. **Install a Linux distribution:** You can choose from several Linux distributions available on the Microsoft Store or use the `wsl --install` command to install a default distribution (e.g., Ubuntu).

Managing Linux Distributions

Once you have WSL set up, you can manage your Linux distributions conveniently:

- **Installing a distribution:** Use the Microsoft Store or the `wsl --install` command followed by the desired distribution name (e.g., `wsl --install -d Ubuntu`).

- **Listing installed distributions:** Run `wsl --list` to see a list of all installed distributions on your system.

- **Setting the default distribution:** You can set a default distribution using `wsl --set-default <DistributionName>`.

- **Launching a distribution:** Simply type the distribution name (e.g., `wsl` or `wsl -d Ubuntu`) in the command prompt to launch it.

Working with Linux in WSL

WSL allows you to work with Linux just like you would on a native Linux machine. You can use the terminal to run Linux commands, install software from repositories, and even develop applications. Here are some common tasks:

- **Updating packages:** Use `sudo apt update` followed by `sudo apt upgrade` to update packages in Ubuntu and other Debian-based distributions. For distributions like CentOS, use `sudo yum update`.

- **Installing software:** Use your distribution's package manager (apt, yum, etc.) to install software. For example, `sudo apt install <package-name>`.

- **Accessing Linux files:** You can access your Windows files from the Linux file system, usually under /mnt/. For example, your C: drive can be found at /mnt/c/.

- **Running graphical applications:** You can run Linux graphical applications by installing an X server for Windows, such as VcXsrv, and configuring WSL to use it. This allows you to run applications with a graphical user interface.

- **Customizing your Linux environment:** You can customize your Linux distribution by editing configuration files, installing shell extensions, and setting up your favorite development tools.

WSL brings the power of Linux to your Windows machine, making it a versatile development and productivity environment. Whether you're a developer, system administrator, or just a Linux enthusiast, WSL provides a seamless experience for working with Linux alongside your Windows 11 setup.

Section 14.3: Managing Virtual Machines with Hyper-V

Hyper-V is a virtualization platform included with Windows 11 that enables you to create and manage virtual machines (VMs) on your computer. It's a powerful tool for various use cases, including software development, testing, running multiple operating systems, and creating isolated environments. In this section, we'll explore how to set up and manage virtual machines using Hyper-V.

Enabling Hyper-V

Before you can start using Hyper-V, you need to ensure that it's enabled on your Windows 11 system. Here's how to enable Hyper-V:

1. **Check System Requirements:** Verify that your computer's hardware supports virtualization technology. Your CPU must support virtualization extensions (e.g., Intel VT-x or AMD-V), and these features should be enabled in your computer's BIOS/UEFI settings.

2. **Enable Hyper-V Feature:** Open PowerShell as an administrator and run the following command to enable the Hyper-V feature:

   ```
   dism.exe /online /enable-feature /featurename:Microsoft-Hyper-V-All /All /norestart
   ```

   This command installs all Hyper-V components.

3. **Reboot Your Computer:** After enabling Hyper-V, you'll need to restart your computer for the changes to take effect.

Creating Virtual Machines

Once Hyper-V is enabled, you can create virtual machines. Here's how to do it:

1. **Open Hyper-V Manager:** You can find it by searching for "Hyper-V Manager" in the Start menu.

2. **Connect to Hyper-V:** If you don't see any servers listed in Hyper-V Manager, you can connect to the local Hyper-V server on your computer.

3. **Create a New Virtual Machine:** Right-click on your server in Hyper-V Manager, select "New," and then choose "Virtual Machine." Follow the wizard to create a new VM.

   – **Specify Name and Location:** Give your VM a name and specify where you want to store its files.

   – **Assign Memory:** Allocate the amount of RAM you want to assign to the VM.

   – **Configure Networking:** Choose a network switch or create a new one to connect your VM to the network.

   – **Connect Virtual Hard Disk:** Create a new virtual hard disk or use an existing one.

   – **Complete the Wizard:** Review your settings and click "Finish" to create the VM.

4. **Install an Operating System:** After creating the VM, you'll need to install an operating system on it. You can attach an ISO file or installation media to the VM and start it to begin the OS installation process.

Managing Virtual Machines

Hyper-V Manager provides various options for managing your virtual machines:

- **Start and Stop VMs:** Right-click on a VM and select "Start" or "Stop" to control its power state.

- **Snapshot and Checkpoints:** You can create snapshots of your VM's current state or checkpoints to save its configuration at a specific point in time.

- **Import and Export VMs:** You can import and export VMs to move them between different Hyper-V hosts.

- **Virtual Switches:** You can create and manage virtual switches to control network connectivity for your VMs.

- **Integration Services:** These are drivers and services that enhance VM performance and integration with the host system.

Using PowerShell for Automation

Hyper-V can also be managed using PowerShell, which is useful for automating tasks and managing VMs programmatically. You can use cmdlets like `New-VM`, `Start-VM`, and `Stop-VM` to perform various actions on virtual machines.

Here's a basic example of creating a new VM using PowerShell:

```
New-VM -Name "MyVM" -MemoryStartupBytes 4GB -NewVHDPath "C:\VMs\MyVM.vhdx" -N
ewVHDSizeBytes 100GB
```

This command creates a new VM named "MyVM" with 4GB of RAM and a 100GB virtual hard disk.

Hyper-V is a versatile tool for managing virtual machines in Windows 11, and it provides a flexible environment for various tasks. Whether you're a developer, tester, or IT administrator, understanding how to use Hyper-V can be a valuable skill for working with virtualization.

Section 14.4: Tips for Efficiently Running Multiple Operating Systems

Running multiple operating systems on a single computer can be incredibly useful, whether you need to test software across different platforms, run legacy applications, or just explore various operating systems. In this section, we'll explore some tips and best practices for efficiently running multiple operating systems using virtualization tools like Hyper-V on Windows 11.

1. Allocate Adequate Resources

When setting up virtual machines (VMs) for different operating systems, make sure to allocate sufficient resources to each VM. This includes CPU cores, RAM, and storage. Overcommitting resources can lead to poor performance and sluggishness in all your VMs. Balance resource allocation based on the specific needs of each OS.

2. Use SSD Storage

If possible, store your virtual hard disks (VHDs) on a solid-state drive (SSD). SSDs provide faster read and write speeds compared to traditional hard drives, which can significantly improve the performance of your VMs, especially during boot times and file operations.

3. Keep VMs Updated

Just like physical machines, VMs need regular updates for security and performance improvements. Make sure to keep your virtual machines up to date by installing OS updates and patches. Most operating systems offer automatic update options.

4. Take Snapshots or Checkpoints

Before making major changes or installations within a VM, take snapshots or checkpoints of its current state. This allows you to roll back to a previous state if something goes wrong. It's an excellent safety net for testing and experimentation.

5. Organize Your VMs

As you accumulate multiple VMs, it's easy to lose track of them. Organize your VMs with clear and descriptive names. Consider creating folders or categories to group related VMs together, making it easier to find and manage them.

6. Use Linked Clones (If Supported)

Some virtualization platforms support linked clones or differencing disks. These allow you to create new VMs that share the same base image, reducing storage requirements. It's particularly useful when you need multiple instances of the same OS.

7. Optimize Startup and Shutdown

Configure your VMs to start up and shut down efficiently. For example, you can set VMs to start up when your host machine boots or only when needed. Similarly, automate the graceful shutdown of VMs when not in use to conserve resources.

8. Backup VMs Regularly

Don't forget to back up your VMs regularly. While snapshots and checkpoints provide a level of protection, it's essential to have full backups of your VMs in case of catastrophic failures or data corruption.

9. Secure Your VMs

Apply the same security practices to your VMs as you would to physical machines. Install antivirus software, enable firewalls, and keep the operating systems and software up to date with security patches. Isolate VMs from each other if they contain sensitive or critical data.

10. Experiment Safely

Virtualization allows you to experiment with different operating systems and configurations. Use this flexibility to your advantage, but be cautious when testing potentially risky configurations. Always have backups or snapshots to revert to a stable state if something goes wrong.

11. Explore Virtual Appliances

Virtual appliance images are pre-configured VMs with specific software or services. They can save you time and effort when setting up complex environments. Many open-source and commercial virtual appliances are available for various purposes.

Running multiple operating systems within virtual machines offers a convenient and efficient way to achieve various tasks. By following these tips, you can ensure that your virtualized environments remain stable, performant, and secure, whether you're a developer, IT professional, or simply a curious explorer of different operating systems.

Section 14.5: Best Practices for Virtualization Security

Virtualization has become a cornerstone of modern IT infrastructure, enabling organizations to efficiently manage resources, improve scalability, and enhance disaster recovery. However, along with its many advantages, virtualization introduces unique security challenges that need to be addressed to maintain a secure computing environment. In this section, we'll explore best practices for virtualization security in the context of Windows 11 and its virtualization tools like Hyper-V.

1. Hypervisor Security

The hypervisor, the core component of virtualization, must be securely configured and regularly patched. Ensure that you apply the latest security updates to your hypervisor, as vulnerabilities in this critical layer can have severe consequences.

2. Isolation of VMs

Each virtual machine (VM) should be isolated from others. This means configuring network and storage access controls to prevent unauthorized communication between VMs. Implement VLANs, firewalls, and access controls to restrict lateral movement within your virtualized environment.

3. Regular Updates

Keep both the host operating system (Windows 11) and guest operating systems (VMs) up to date with security patches and updates. Vulnerabilities in guest VMs can be exploited to compromise the entire virtualization infrastructure.

4. Use Virtual Trusted Platform Module (vTPM)

If your virtualization platform supports it, enable a virtual Trusted Platform Module (vTPM) in VMs that require secure boot and encryption. This can enhance the security of VMs by providing hardware-based security features.

5. Resource Monitoring and Allocation

Implement resource monitoring to detect abnormal resource consumption patterns that may indicate malicious activity or compromised VMs. Allocate resources based on workload requirements to prevent resource contention and ensure fair resource distribution.

6. Backup and Disaster Recovery

Maintain regular backups of critical VMs and configurations. This is essential for disaster recovery in case of hardware failures, data corruption, or security incidents. Test your backup and recovery procedures to ensure they work effectively.

7. Security Groups and Policies

Leverage security groups and policies within your virtualization platform to enforce security controls at the virtual network level. Create security policies that restrict unnecessary communication and access between VMs.

8. Virtual Networking Security

Segment virtual networks and apply network security controls to prevent unauthorized access. Implement network intrusion detection and prevention systems (NIDS/NIPS) to monitor and block malicious network traffic.

9. Guest VM Security

Apply security best practices within guest VMs, including regular patching, antivirus software, firewalls, and proper user access controls. Guest VMs should be treated with the same security diligence as physical machines.

10. Host Hardening

Harden the host operating system (Windows 11) to reduce its attack surface. Disable unnecessary services and features, apply host-based firewalls, and regularly review and audit host configurations.

11. Access Control

Implement strong access controls for virtualization management interfaces and consoles. Use multi-factor authentication (MFA) where possible and restrict access to only authorized personnel.

12. Security Monitoring and Logging

Enable comprehensive logging for your virtualization infrastructure. Regularly review logs for signs of suspicious activities and incidents. Consider using a centralized log management solution for better visibility.

13. Security Training

Ensure that your IT staff and administrators receive adequate training in virtualization security. Knowledgeable personnel are essential for effectively managing and securing virtual environments.

14. Incident Response Plan

Develop an incident response plan specific to virtualization security incidents. This plan should include procedures for detecting, isolating, and mitigating security breaches in your virtualized environment.

15. Regular Security Audits

Perform regular security audits and assessments of your virtualization infrastructure. These audits should evaluate the effectiveness of your security controls and identify areas for improvement.

By following these best practices, you can enhance the security of your virtualized environment in Windows 11. Virtualization offers numerous benefits, but it's essential to proactively address security concerns to protect your data and infrastructure from threats and vulnerabilities.

Chapter 15: Integrating with Mobile Devices

Section 15.1: Linking Your Phone with Windows 11

In the modern world, our smartphones have become an integral part of our lives, serving as communication devices, personal organizers, and sources of entertainment. Windows 11 recognizes this and offers seamless integration with your mobile phone, allowing you to link your phone to your PC for a more cohesive experience. In this section, we'll explore how to link your phone with Windows 11 and the benefits it brings.

Why Link Your Phone with Windows 11?

Linking your phone with Windows 11 offers several advantages:

1. **Cross-Device Continuity:** You can start a task on your phone and finish it on your Windows 11 PC, and vice versa. This continuity enhances your productivity.

2. **Notifications Sync:** Your phone's notifications, including text messages, calls, and app notifications, can appear on your PC, ensuring you don't miss anything important.

3. **Easy File Sharing:** Quickly share files and photos between your phone and PC without needing to connect cables or use third-party apps.

4. **Phone Calls from Your PC:** Make and receive calls from your PC using your phone's connection. This feature is handy when your phone is charging or not within reach.

How to Link Your Phone with Windows 11

Here's a step-by-step guide to linking your phone with Windows 11:

1. **Open Settings:** Click on the **Start Menu** and then the **Settings** gear icon.

2. **Go to Phone Settings:** In the Settings window, click on the **Phone** option.

3. **Add a Phone:** Under the Phone settings, click on the **Add a Phone** button.

4. **Follow the Prompts:** Windows will guide you through the process of linking your phone. This typically involves installing the "Your Phone" app on your mobile device and signing in with your Microsoft account.

5. **Complete the Setup:** Once the setup is complete, your phone will be linked to your Windows 11 PC.

Using Linked Features

After linking your phone, you can use various linked features:

- **Notifications:** Your phone's notifications will appear in the Windows 11 Action Center. You can respond to text messages and even make calls directly from your PC.

- **Your Phone App:** The "Your Phone" app on your PC allows you to access your phone's photos, messages, and notifications.

- **Cross-Device Copy and Paste:** Copy text or files on one device and paste them on another seamlessly.

- **Phone Screen Mirroring:** Some Android devices support screen mirroring, allowing you to view and interact with your phone's screen on your PC.

- **Link to Windows for Samsung Devices:** If you have a Samsung device, you can use the "Link to Windows" feature for deeper integration.

Privacy and Security

Microsoft takes privacy and security seriously. When you link your phone, you have control over which features and data are shared between your devices. You can customize these settings in the "Your Phone" app and Windows 11 settings.

In summary, linking your phone with Windows 11 enhances your productivity and streamlines your digital life. It's a feature that brings your PC and mobile device closer, allowing you to seamlessly switch between them and access your phone's content and capabilities directly from your computer.

Section 15.2: Managing Notifications and Continuity Between Devices

After linking your phone with Windows 11, you'll experience a new level of continuity between your PC and mobile device. One of the key aspects of this integration is the management of notifications. In this section, we'll delve into how you can effectively manage notifications and ensure a seamless flow of information between your devices.

Notification Sync Across Devices

One of the primary benefits of linking your phone with Windows 11 is the synchronization of notifications. When you receive a notification on your mobile device, it can also appear on your Windows 11 PC. This feature ensures that you stay informed and don't miss any important updates, whether it's a text message, an email, or an app notification.

Managing Notification Settings

To make the most of this feature, you can customize notification settings:

1. **Open Settings:** Click on the **Start Menu** and then the **Settings** gear icon.

2. **Go to System Settings:** In the Settings window, click on **System**.

3. **Choose Notifications & Actions:** On the left sidebar, select **Notifications & Actions**.

4. **Sync Notifications:** Scroll down to find the **Phone** section. Here, you can enable or disable notification syncing between your phone and PC.

5. **Adjust Other Settings:** You can also configure notification-related settings such as the number of notifications visible in the Action Center and whether notifications are accompanied by sounds.

Responding to Notifications

When a notification appears on your Windows 11 PC, you can interact with it just like you would on your phone:

- **Reply to Text Messages:** If it's a text message notification, you can reply directly from your PC without picking up your phone.

- **Answer Calls:** For incoming calls, you can choose to accept or decline the call right from your PC.

- **View App Notifications:** App notifications will display on your PC, allowing you to open the associated app or dismiss the notification.

Notification History

Windows 11 also offers a feature called Notification History, which allows you to review past notifications:

1. **Open Settings:** Navigate to **Settings > Privacy & Security > Notifications**.

2. **Enable Notification History:** Toggle on the **Notification History** option.

3. **View Past Notifications:** Once enabled, you can access your notification history by clicking the clock icon in the lower-right corner of the taskbar.

Maintaining Privacy

While notification syncing is convenient, it's important to maintain your privacy. You can choose which apps can send notifications to your PC and customize notification settings on a per-app basis.

Wrapping Up

Managing notifications and ensuring continuity between your phone and Windows 11 PC is a powerful feature that enhances your overall experience. It keeps you connected and productive, allowing you to seamlessly switch between devices and stay updated with important information. By customizing notification settings to your preferences, you can make this feature work best for you while maintaining your privacy.

Section 15.3: Using Your Phone App for Calls, Texts, and Photos

The integration between Windows 11 and your mobile phone extends beyond notifications. You can use the "Your Phone" app to perform various tasks, such as making and receiving calls, sending and receiving text messages, and accessing photos stored on your mobile device. This section explores the capabilities of the "Your Phone" app and how it enhances your cross-device experience.

Setting Up Your Phone

Before you can use the "Your Phone" app, you need to set it up for the first time:

1. **Install the App:** If you haven't already, download and install the "Your Phone" app from the Microsoft Store on your Windows 11 PC.

2. **Link Your Phone:** Launch the app and follow the on-screen instructions to link your mobile device. You'll need to install the "Your Phone Companion" app on your phone, available on both Android and iOS.

3. **Permissions:** Grant the necessary permissions for the app to access your phone's features.

Once set up, you'll have access to several features that bridge the gap between your PC and mobile device.

Making and Receiving Calls

One of the standout features of the "Your Phone" app is the ability to make and receive calls from your PC. Here's how:

- **Initiating a Call:** Open the "Your Phone" app on your PC, click the "Calls" tab, and select "New call." You can enter a phone number or choose a contact from your synced phone.

- **Answering Calls:** When you receive an incoming call on your mobile device, a notification will appear on your PC. You can answer or decline the call from your PC.

This feature is handy when your phone is not within arm's reach or if you prefer the convenience of your PC.

Sending and Receiving Text Messages

You can also send and receive text messages through the "Your Phone" app:

- **Sending a Text:** In the app, navigate to the "Messages" tab, click "New message," and select a contact or enter a phone number. Type your message, and hit send.

- **Receiving Messages:** When you receive a text message on your phone, it will appear in the app on your PC, allowing you to respond without switching devices.

Accessing Photos

The "Your Phone" app simplifies the process of accessing photos from your mobile device on your PC:

- **Photos Tab:** Open the "Photos" tab in the app to view and manage your mobile device's photos.

- **Drag and Drop:** You can drag and drop photos from the app to your PC or vice versa, making it easy to transfer images between devices.

Maintaining Connectivity

To ensure a seamless experience with the "Your Phone" app, make sure both your PC and mobile device are connected to the same Wi-Fi network and have Bluetooth enabled. Additionally, keeping both devices updated with the latest software and app versions is essential for optimal performance.

Wrapping Up

The "Your Phone" app in Windows 11 enhances your productivity and connectivity by enabling you to make calls, send texts, and access photos from your mobile device directly on your PC. It streamlines the interaction between your devices, allowing you to stay focused and efficient without the need to constantly switch between screens. Whether you're working, communicating, or sharing photos, this app makes it easier to manage your digital life across devices.

Section 15.4: Synchronizing Files and Settings Across Devices

Windows 11 offers robust features for synchronizing files and settings across your various devices, including PCs, tablets, and smartphones. This synchronization not only ensures that you have access to your essential data from any device but also helps in maintaining a consistent user experience. In this section, we will explore how to set up and make the most of this synchronization.

Microsoft Account: The Key to Syncing

To begin syncing your files and settings across devices, you need to use a Microsoft account. If you're using Windows 11, you likely already have one, but you can create a new one if needed. Your Microsoft account serves as the bridge that connects your devices and ensures that your data stays up to date.

Syncing Settings

Windows 11 allows you to synchronize various settings across devices:

- **Themes and Personalization:** Your desktop background, theme colors, and even the layout of the Start menu can sync between your devices. This ensures a consistent visual experience.

- **Passwords:** If you use Microsoft Edge as your browser, your saved passwords can sync, making it easier to log in to websites from any device.

- **Language Preferences:** Language and input preferences, including keyboard layouts, can sync. This is especially useful if you use multiple languages.

- **Accessibility Settings:** If you have specific accessibility settings configured, such as text size or narrator settings, they can sync across devices.

- **App Settings:** Some Windows apps support syncing settings. For example, the Mail app can sync email account settings.

To ensure that these settings sync, make sure the "Sync settings" option is turned on in your Windows settings:

1. Open **Settings** by pressing Win + I.

2. Go to **Accounts** and select **Sync your settings**.

3. Toggle on the switches for the settings you want to sync.

Syncing Files with OneDrive

OneDrive is Microsoft's cloud storage service, and it seamlessly integrates with Windows 11 to keep your files synchronized. Here's how to set it up:

1. **Sign In to OneDrive:** Ensure you're signed in to your Microsoft account on Windows 11.

2. **Enable OneDrive:** Open the OneDrive app from the Start menu and sign in if prompted. It will create a OneDrive folder in your File Explorer.

3. **Add Files to OneDrive:** To sync files and folders, move them into the OneDrive folder. These files will be accessible from any device with OneDrive and will stay updated automatically.

4. **Access Anywhere:** You can access your OneDrive files through the OneDrive website or the OneDrive app on your mobile device.

Cross-Device App Installs

The Microsoft Store also supports cross-device app installations. When you install an app from the Microsoft Store on one device, you can choose to install it on other devices associated with your Microsoft account. This feature is particularly useful for maintaining consistency in your app ecosystem.

Troubleshooting Sync Issues

If you encounter synchronization issues, ensure that your devices are connected to the internet and signed in to the same Microsoft account. Sometimes, delays in synchronization can occur due to network conditions. Additionally, make sure your devices have the latest Windows updates installed.

Privacy and Security Considerations

While synchronization is convenient, it's crucial to consider the privacy and security aspects. Ensure that your Microsoft account is protected with a strong password and two-factor authentication. Be mindful of what you choose to sync, especially if you share your devices with others.

Conclusion

Synchronizing files and settings across devices in Windows 11 streamlines your digital life and ensures a consistent experience. By utilizing a Microsoft account, enabling OneDrive, and configuring sync settings, you can seamlessly access your data and preferences from any Windows 11 device. It's a powerful feature that enhances productivity and convenience, making your Windows experience truly versatile.

Section 15.5: Remote Access and Management of Mobile Devices

In an increasingly interconnected world, the ability to access and manage your mobile devices remotely is a valuable asset. Windows 11 provides features that allow you to connect to and control your mobile devices, whether they are smartphones or tablets, from your PC. This section explores how to establish remote access and manage your mobile devices efficiently.

Your Phone App: A Gateway to Your Mobile World

The "Your Phone" app in Windows 11 is the key to integrating your mobile devices with your PC. With this app, you can sync notifications, messages, photos, and even make and receive calls from your phone on your PC. Here's how to set it up:

1. **Check Device Compatibility:** Make sure your Android or iOS device is compatible with the Your Phone app. Android devices offer more features, while iOS devices have limited functionality.

2. **Download the Your Phone App:** If it's not already installed, download the Your Phone app from the Microsoft Store on your Windows 11 PC.

3. **Connect Your Mobile Device:**

- For Android: Follow the on-screen instructions to connect your Android device using the Your Phone Companion app from the Google Play Store.
- For iOS: Install the Your Phone Companion app on your iOS device, then follow the setup instructions on your PC.

4. **Access Your Mobile Apps:** Once connected, you can access your mobile apps on your PC. They will appear in the "Apps" section of the Your Phone app.

5. **Sync Messages and Notifications:** You can also read and reply to text messages, view photos, and receive mobile notifications directly on your PC.

Making and Receiving Calls from Your PC

One of the standout features of the Your Phone app is the ability to make and receive calls from your PC using your mobile device's number. To set this up:

1. Ensure your mobile device is connected to the Your Phone app.

2. In the Your Phone app on your PC, go to the "Calls" section.

3. You'll see a list of your recent calls, and you can make new calls by dialing numbers or selecting contacts.

4. When you receive a call on your mobile device, you'll see a notification on your PC, and you can answer the call directly from your computer.

Drag-and-Drop File Transfer

With the Your Phone app, you can also transfer files between your PC and mobile device using a simple drag-and-drop method. This feature is handy for quickly sharing photos, documents, and other files between your devices.

Remote Desktop

While the Your Phone app offers convenience for managing mobile devices, Windows 11 also provides a more comprehensive solution for remote access through the built-in Remote Desktop feature. This feature allows you to connect to another Windows PC or mobile device and control it as if you were physically present.

To use Remote Desktop:

1. **Enable Remote Desktop:** On the device you want to control remotely, go to Settings > System > Remote Desktop. Turn on Remote Desktop, and note down the PC's name or IP address.

2. **Connect from Your Windows 11 PC:** On your Windows 11 PC, open the Remote Desktop app. Enter the name or IP address of the remote device and follow the prompts to connect.

3. **Control Your Device:** Once connected, you can control the remote device, access its files, and run applications as if you were sitting in front of it.

Privacy and Security Considerations

When using remote access features, security is paramount. Ensure that you use strong, unique passwords for your Microsoft account and mobile devices. Enable two-factor authentication where possible.

For remote desktop access, always connect to trusted devices, and don't share access with anyone you don't trust. Use secure, private networks when accessing your devices remotely to protect your data.

Conclusion

Remote access and management of mobile devices are essential capabilities in today's interconnected world. With Windows 11, you have powerful tools at your disposal through the Your Phone app and Remote Desktop feature. These tools not only enhance your productivity but also allow you to stay connected and in control, even when you're away from your mobile devices.

Chapter 16: Exploring Advanced Features

Section 16.1: Utilizing Widgets for At-a-Glance Information

In Windows 11, Widgets provide a convenient way to access at-a-glance information, personalized news, weather updates, calendar events, and more. Widgets are designed to enhance your productivity by quickly providing you with relevant information without the need to open multiple applications. In this section, we'll explore how to make the most of Widgets in Windows 11.

Widgets can be accessed by clicking on the Widgets icon in the taskbar or by using the keyboard shortcut Win + W. Once opened, you'll see a variety of Widgets displayed on the left side of your screen. You can customize which Widgets appear by clicking on the "Add Widgets" button.

Widgets can be grouped into various categories such as News, Calendar, Weather, To-Do, and more. You can rearrange and resize Widgets on your screen to suit your preferences. To rearrange a Widget, simply click and drag it to the desired position. To resize a Widget, click on the bottom-right corner and drag it to adjust its size.

One of the most useful Widgets is the News Widget. It provides you with personalized news articles based on your interests and preferences. You can configure your interests in the News Widget settings to receive news updates on topics that matter to you.

The Weather Widget is another handy tool that provides real-time weather information for your location. You can add multiple locations to track weather conditions in different areas.

If you're someone who relies on their calendar to stay organized, the Calendar Widget is a valuable addition. It displays your upcoming events and appointments, ensuring you never miss an important meeting or deadline.

Widgets can also be used to control media playback, including audio and video. You can control playback, adjust volume, and skip tracks without leaving the Widget interface.

To further personalize your Widgets experience, you can choose from various Widgets available in the Microsoft Store. These additional Widgets can cater to specific interests, hobbies, or productivity needs.

Widgets in Windows 11 are designed to provide quick access to information and improve your workflow. By customizing and organizing Widgets to your liking, you can stay informed and efficient while working on your computer.

In the next section, we'll explore advanced gestures and touchpad features in Windows 11, enhancing your interaction with the operating system even further.

Section 16.2: Advanced Gestures and Touchpad Features

Windows 11 introduces advanced touchpad gestures and features that make navigating your computer more intuitive and efficient. These touchpad enhancements provide a seamless and responsive way to interact with your device, especially on laptops and 2-in-1 devices. In this section, we'll explore some of the advanced gestures and touchpad settings available in Windows 11.

Basic Touchpad Gestures

Before diving into advanced gestures, let's review some basic touchpad gestures that are fundamental to using Windows 11:

1. **Single-Finger Tap**: A single tap on the touchpad simulates a left-click, allowing you to select items, open applications, and perform various actions.

2. **Single-Finger Tap and Hold**: Tap and hold for a moment to initiate a right-click, which opens context menus and additional options.

3. **Two-Finger Scroll**: Place two fingers on the touchpad and move them up or down to scroll through documents, web pages, or lists.

4. **Two-Finger Pinch**: Pinch two fingers together or spread them apart to zoom in or out on content, such as images and web pages.

5. **Three-Finger Swipe**: Swipe horizontally or vertically with three fingers to switch between open applications or virtual desktops.

Advanced Touchpad Gestures

Windows 11 extends touchpad functionality with advanced gestures:

1. **Three-Finger Tap**: A three-finger tap opens the Search menu, making it easy to find files, apps, and settings quickly.

2. **Four-Finger Swipe**: Swipe horizontally with four fingers to switch between open applications. This gesture provides a smooth way to navigate your multitasking environment.

3. **Four-Finger Tap**: Tapping with four fingers opens the Action Center, where you can access notifications, quick settings, and other system functions.

4. **Precision Touchpad Settings**: Windows 11 offers precision touchpad settings that allow you to customize sensitivity, gestures, and scrolling behavior to suit your preferences. To access these settings, go to "Settings" > "Devices" > "Touchpad."

Multitasking with Touchpad Gestures

Windows 11 enhances multitasking with touchpad gestures:

1. **Snap Layouts**: To quickly organize open windows, use a three-finger swipe up to access Snap Layouts. These layouts allow you to arrange windows side by side or in a grid for improved productivity.

2. **Snap Groups**: With a three-finger swipe down, you can access Snap Groups, which display all your open apps within a group for easy switching between related tasks.

Customizing Touchpad Gestures

You can customize touchpad gestures to match your workflow:

1. **Custom Gestures**: Windows 11 allows you to create custom touchpad gestures to perform specific actions or launch applications. This feature can be found in touchpad settings.

2. **Adjusting Sensitivity**: If you find the touchpad too sensitive or not responsive enough, you can fine-tune its sensitivity in touchpad settings.

3. **Scrolling Options**: Customize how the touchpad handles scrolling, including the direction and speed of scrolling, to match your preferences.

4. **Three-Finger Drag**: Enable three-finger drag to move windows around the screen easily. It's particularly useful for users who prefer this method of window management.

By mastering these advanced touchpad gestures and customization options, you can significantly improve your Windows 11 experience on devices with precision touchpads. Whether you're working, browsing, or multitasking, these gestures can streamline your interactions and boost your productivity.

Section 16.3: Exploring Spatial Sound and Advanced Audio Features

Windows 11 comes with a range of advanced audio features that enhance your listening experience and provide immersive sound quality. One such feature is Spatial Sound, which allows you to perceive audio in three dimensions, making it feel as if sound is coming from different directions. In this section, we'll explore Spatial Sound and other advanced audio options available in Windows 11.

Spatial Sound

Spatial Sound is a technology that simulates 3D audio by creating an immersive soundstage around you. This technology can be particularly captivating when watching movies, playing games, or listening to music. Windows 11 offers several spatial sound formats, including Windows Sonic, Dolby Atmos, and DTS:X.

Enabling Spatial Sound

To enable Spatial Sound in Windows 11:

1. Right-click on the sound icon in the taskbar and select "Spatial Sound."

2. Choose your preferred spatial sound format (e.g., Windows Sonic, Dolby Atmos, or DTS:X).

3. Click "Apply" to enable the selected format.

Benefits of Spatial Sound

- **Immersive Gaming**: In games that support spatial sound, you can hear audio cues and effects as if they are coming from specific directions. This enhances your gaming experience and can provide a competitive edge.

- **Cinematic Experience**: When watching movies or videos with spatial sound, you'll feel like you're in the middle of the action, with sound coming from various directions for a more lifelike experience.

Audio Enhancements

Windows 11 offers various audio enhancements that cater to different listening preferences:

Equalizer

The Equalizer allows you to adjust the balance of audio frequencies to suit your taste. You can fine-tune the bass, treble, and other aspects of audio output. To access the Equalizer:

1. Right-click on the sound icon in the taskbar and select "Open Sound settings."

2. Scroll down to the "Advanced sound options" section and click on "App volume and device preferences."

3. Under "Other sound options," click on "Equalizer" to access the settings.

Enhancements

Windows 11 provides audio enhancements to improve sound quality:

- **Bass Boost**: This enhances low-frequency audio, making music and movie explosions more impactful.

- **Virtual Surround**: It creates a virtual surround sound experience with stereo headphones.

- **Loudness Equalization**: This feature equalizes the volume levels of different audio sources, so you don't have to constantly adjust the volume.

- **Room Correction**: It adjusts audio output to compensate for your room's acoustics, improving sound quality.

You can explore and enable these audio enhancements in the "Sound" settings of Windows 11.

Advanced Audio Devices

Windows 11 supports a wide range of audio devices, including external DACs (digital-to-analog converters) and headphones with advanced audio processing capabilities. If you have such devices, you can access their specific settings and features through the "Sound" settings.

Dolby Atmos for Headphones

Dolby Atmos for Headphones is a premium audio experience that delivers three-dimensional sound on compatible headphones. You can enable and configure this feature in the "Sound" settings.

In conclusion, Windows 11 offers a rich array of audio features, from spatial sound to customizable equalizers and audio enhancements. These features cater to both casual users and audiophiles, ensuring that you can enjoy high-quality audio tailored to your preferences. Whether you're gaming, watching movies, or listening to music, Windows 11's advanced audio capabilities can elevate your overall experience.

Section 16.4: Leveraging AI and Machine Learning Features in Windows 11

Windows 11 incorporates artificial intelligence (AI) and machine learning (ML) features that enhance various aspects of the operating system. These technologies are designed to make your experience more personalized, efficient, and productive. In this section, we'll explore some of the AI and ML features in Windows 11.

1. Windows Hello Facial Recognition

Windows Hello is an AI-driven biometric authentication feature in Windows 11 that allows you to log in to your computer using facial recognition. It uses deep learning algorithms to recognize your face quickly and securely. To set up Windows Hello:

1. Go to "Settings" > "Accounts" > "Sign-in options."

2. Under "Windows Hello Face," click on "Set up" and follow the on-screen instructions.

Once set up, you can log in by simply looking at your computer's camera, providing a seamless and secure login experience.

2. AI-Powered Virtual Assistant: Cortana

Cortana, Microsoft's virtual assistant, is now powered by AI and ML algorithms, making it smarter and more helpful. Cortana can assist you with tasks, answer questions, set reminders, and even predict your needs based on your usage patterns. You can access Cortana by clicking the microphone icon in the taskbar or using the "Hey Cortana" voice command.

3. AI-Based Predictive Typing: Text Suggestions

Windows 11's on-screen keyboard features AI-driven text suggestions that make typing on touchscreens and tablets faster and more accurate. As you type, the AI predicts the next word or phrase you intend to type, allowing you to tap the suggested word instead of typing it out fully.

4. AI-Enhanced Search

The Windows 11 search function is now powered by AI, providing more accurate and context-aware results. As you use the search bar in the taskbar, Windows learns your search habits and adapts its results to become more relevant over time. This feature improves the efficiency of finding files, applications, and settings.

5. AI-Powered App Recommendations

Windows 11 uses AI to recommend apps from the Microsoft Store based on your usage patterns and interests. These recommendations can help you discover new apps that are relevant to your needs and preferences.

6. AI-Enhanced Battery Management

For laptops and portable devices, Windows 11 incorporates AI-driven battery management. It learns your usage patterns and optimizes power settings to extend battery life. This feature can be especially useful when you're on the go and need to maximize your device's battery performance.

7. AI-Driven Updates and Maintenance

Windows 11 uses AI to schedule system updates and maintenance tasks intelligently. It analyzes your usage patterns and ensures that updates and maintenance activities do not disrupt your workflow. This helps keep your system up to date and secure without inconveniencing you.

8. AI-Enhanced Voice Recognition

Voice recognition in Windows 11 benefits from AI algorithms that improve accuracy and understanding. Whether you're using voice commands to control your computer or dictating text, the AI-driven voice recognition makes these interactions more reliable and efficient.

9. AI-Based Gaming Enhancements

In the realm of gaming, Windows 11 leverages AI to enhance graphics, improve frame rates, and reduce latency. Features like DirectX 12 Ultimate and Auto HDR use machine learning to deliver a more immersive gaming experience.

In conclusion, Windows 11's integration of AI and machine learning features extends across various aspects of the operating system, from authentication and virtual assistance to predictive typing and gaming enhancements. These features aim to provide a more personalized, efficient, and enjoyable computing experience, making Windows 11 a powerful and intelligent platform for users of all kinds.

Section 16.5: Advanced Graphic Features for Professional Use

Windows 11 offers advanced graphic features that cater to professional users, including designers, video editors, and 3D artists. These features are designed to provide a seamless and efficient environment for graphic-intensive tasks. In this section, we will explore some of the advanced graphic features available in Windows 11.

1. DirectX 12 Ultimate

Windows 11 includes support for DirectX 12 Ultimate, which is the latest iteration of Microsoft's graphics API. DirectX 12 Ultimate brings advanced graphics technologies, including ray tracing, mesh shaders, and variable-rate shading. These technologies allow game developers and content creators to achieve higher levels of realism, detail, and performance in their work.

2. Auto HDR

Auto High Dynamic Range (HDR) is a feature that enhances the visual quality of games and applications. With Auto HDR, Windows 11 automatically adds HDR enhancements to games that support it, even if your monitor is not HDR-compatible. This feature results in more vibrant colors, improved contrast, and a better overall visual experience.

3. DirectStorage

DirectStorage is a feature that significantly reduces load times in games and applications. It leverages the speed of modern NVMe SSDs to load assets and textures directly from storage, bypassing traditional storage bottlenecks. This results in faster loading of large game worlds and improved overall performance.

4. Professional-Grade Color Management

For professionals who require precise color reproduction, Windows 11 offers advanced color management features. You can calibrate your display to ensure accurate color representation, and the operating system supports a wide range of color spaces, including sRGB, DCI-P3, and Adobe RGB.

5. Multiple Monitor Support

Windows 11 provides enhanced support for multiple monitors, making it easier for professionals to set up complex workspaces. You can customize each monitor's resolution, refresh rate, and scaling independently, ensuring a seamless and productive multi-monitor setup.

6. 3D Modeling and Animation Tools

For 3D artists and animators, Windows 11 includes built-in 3D modeling and animation tools. You can create, edit, and animate 3D objects directly within the operating system. Additionally, Windows 11 supports popular 3D file formats, making it compatible with a wide range of 3D design applications.

7. Precision Touch and Pen Input

Windows 11 offers precision touch and pen input support for creative professionals. If you have a touchscreen or stylus-compatible device, you can use it for precise drawing, sketching, and annotation. Windows Ink Workspace provides a dedicated space for pen-based creativity.

8. GPU Performance Metrics

Professionals who rely on GPU performance can benefit from Windows 11's built-in GPU performance metrics. You can monitor GPU utilization, temperature, and other performance metrics in real-time, helping you optimize your workflow and identify potential bottlenecks.

9. Virtual Reality (VR) Integration

For those involved in VR development or content creation, Windows 11 offers seamless VR integration. You can connect and use VR headsets with ease, and the operating system supports VR-ready hardware and software, making it a suitable platform for VR projects.

In conclusion, Windows 11 provides a range of advanced graphic features that cater to the needs of professionals in creative fields and those who require high-performance graphics for gaming and content creation. Whether you're a designer, video editor, or 3D artist, these features enhance your ability to work efficiently and achieve exceptional results on the Windows 11 platform.

Chapter 17: Customizing for Business and Enterprise

In this chapter, we delve into the aspects of customizing Windows 11 for the business and enterprise environments. Windows 11 offers a range of features and tools that cater to the specific needs of businesses, including centralized management, security, and scalability. Section 17.1 focuses on key considerations when deploying Windows 11 in the business environment.

17.1. Windows 11 in the Business Environment: Key Considerations

When implementing Windows 11 within a business or enterprise, there are several critical considerations to keep in mind to ensure a smooth and secure operation. These considerations encompass various aspects, from licensing to management and security.

1. Licensing and Volume Activation

Businesses typically acquire Windows licenses through volume licensing agreements. It's essential to understand the licensing terms and ensure compliance with Microsoft's licensing policies. Volume Activation Services (VAS) can simplify license management and activation across multiple devices.

2. System Requirements and Hardware Compatibility

Before deploying Windows 11, assess the system requirements and hardware compatibility of your existing devices. Ensure that your hardware meets the specifications for Windows 11 to avoid potential compatibility issues.

3. Group Policies and Configuration

Windows 11 provides extensive Group Policy settings that allow administrators to configure and manage various aspects of the operating system. Establish Group Policies that align with your organization's security and operational requirements.

4. Active Directory Integration

Integrating Windows 11 with Active Directory (AD) streamlines user management, authentication, and security policies. Ensure that your AD environment is prepared for Windows 11 integration and leverage AD features for centralized control.

5. Windows Update for Business

Implement a structured approach to Windows updates using Windows Update for Business. Configure update rings, deployment schedules, and feature updates to minimize disruptions and maintain security.

6. Security Features and Endpoint Protection

Windows 11 offers robust security features, including Windows Defender, BitLocker, and Windows Hello. Customize security settings and implement endpoint protection strategies to safeguard business data and devices.

7. Application Compatibility

Evaluate the compatibility of business-critical applications with Windows 11. Work with application vendors to ensure that your software stack is compatible and ready for deployment.

8. Data Backup and Recovery

Implement data backup and recovery solutions to protect critical business data. Windows 11 includes built-in backup tools, but consider third-party solutions for comprehensive data protection.

9. Remote Desktop Services (RDS)

For remote work scenarios, configure Remote Desktop Services (RDS) to enable secure remote access to corporate resources. Implement Virtual Private Networks (VPNs) or DirectAccess for secure connections.

10. Compliance and Data Governance

Adhere to industry-specific compliance requirements and data governance policies. Ensure that Windows 11 configurations and security measures align with regulatory standards.

11. User Training and Support

Provide training and support for end-users to help them adapt to Windows 11. A well-informed user base can contribute to smoother transitions and improved productivity.

12. Disaster Recovery Planning

Develop a comprehensive disaster recovery plan that covers potential Windows 11-related issues. Regularly test and update the plan to address evolving threats and challenges.

In summary, deploying Windows 11 in a business or enterprise environment requires careful planning and consideration of various factors. By addressing licensing, hardware, security, and management aspects, businesses can leverage Windows 11 to enhance productivity, security, and scalability within their organization. Section 17.1 serves as a starting point for businesses looking to embark on their Windows 11 deployment journey.

17.2. Managing Group Policies and Network Settings

Managing Group Policies and network settings is a critical aspect of customizing Windows 11 for business and enterprise environments. Group Policies allow administrators to define and enforce specific configurations and security policies across a network of Windows 11 devices. This section explores the essential considerations and steps involved in managing Group Policies and network settings effectively.

Group Policies (GPOs) Overview

Group Policies are a set of rules and settings that administrators use to control and manage user and computer configurations in an Active Directory environment. GPOs provide a centralized and efficient way to enforce security, compliance, and operational policies across Windows-based networks.

Creating and Managing Group Policies

1. **Accessing Group Policy Management**: To create and manage Group Policies, open the "Group Policy Management Console" (GPMC) on a Windows server computer. You can also manage GPOs on a local machine using the "Local Group Policy Editor" (gpedit.msc).

2. **Creating a GPO**: In the GPMC, navigate to the desired organizational unit (OU) or domain, right-click, and choose "Create a GPO in this domain, and link it here." Give the GPO a descriptive name and click "OK."

3. **Editing GPO Settings**: Right-click on the newly created GPO and choose "Edit" to open the Group Policy Object Editor. Here, you can configure various settings, including security, application management, Windows components, and more.

4. **Linking GPOs**: You can link GPOs to specific OUs, domains, or sites. This determines which users and computers the GPO applies to. Linking allows for targeted policy enforcement.

5. **Enforcing GPOs**: By default, GPOs are inherited from parent containers to child containers. To enforce a specific GPO and prevent inheritance, you can set the "Enforced" option.

Common Group Policy Settings

In a business or enterprise environment, several common Group Policy settings are crucial for managing Windows 11 devices effectively:

1. Security Policies

- **Password Policies**: Enforce password complexity, length, and expiration settings.

- **Account Lockout Policies**: Define lockout thresholds and duration for failed login attempts.
- **Firewall Settings**: Configure Windows Firewall rules and exceptions.
- **BitLocker Policies**: Manage encryption settings for device security.

2. Software Deployment

- **Software Installation**: Deploy and manage software applications across the network using Group Policy-based software distribution.

3. Windows Update Settings

- **Windows Update Policies**: Specify how Windows 11 devices receive and install updates. Use Windows Update for Business for centralized update management.

4. User and Computer Configuration

- **User Configuration**: Customize user profiles, desktop settings, and application configurations.
- **Computer Configuration**: Define system-wide settings, including security, network, and administrative policies.

Network Settings and Security

Managing network settings is integral to ensuring connectivity and security within an enterprise. Here are key considerations:

1. Network Configuration

- **Static IP Addresses**: Assign static IP addresses to servers and critical devices for stability.
- **DHCP Configuration**: Configure DHCP servers to provide dynamic IP addressing to client devices.

2. DNS and Active Directory Integration

- **DNS Settings**: Ensure proper DNS configuration and integration with Active Directory for domain resolution.

3. Virtual Private Networks (VPNs)

- **VPN Setup**: Establish secure VPN connections for remote access and secure data transmission.
- **Network Security**: Implement robust security measures to protect against threats, such as intrusion detection and prevention systems (IDPS).

4. Network Access Control (NAC)

- **NAC Policies**: Define Network Access Control policies to enforce security compliance for devices connecting to the network.

Effective management of Group Policies and network settings plays a pivotal role in maintaining a secure, compliant, and efficient Windows 11 environment for businesses and enterprises. Administrators should regularly review and update policies to adapt to evolving requirements and security threats.

17.3. Advanced Security Features for Business Users

In Windows 11, advanced security features are essential for business users and organizations to protect sensitive data, prevent unauthorized access, and defend against modern cyber threats. This section explores key advanced security features that can be leveraged to enhance security in a business environment.

Windows Defender Advanced Threat Protection (ATP)

Windows Defender ATP is an integrated endpoint security platform that provides comprehensive threat protection, detection, and response capabilities. It helps businesses identify and mitigate advanced threats in real-time.

Key Features:
1. **Endpoint Detection and Response (EDR)**: Windows Defender ATP continuously monitors endpoints for suspicious activities and alerts administrators to potential threats. It provides detailed insights into attack patterns and allows for immediate response actions.

2. **Threat Intelligence**: Windows Defender ATP leverages threat intelligence from Microsoft and industry sources to stay updated on the latest threats and vulnerabilities.

3. **Automated Investigation and Remediation**: The platform can automatically investigate and remediate common security incidents, reducing the burden on IT staff.

4. **Isolation and Quarantine**: Suspicious files or devices can be isolated from the network to prevent the spread of malware.

5. **Threat Analytics**: Windows Defender ATP offers advanced analytics to identify potential security weaknesses and areas that require attention.

Microsoft BitLocker

BitLocker is a disk encryption program that helps protect data on Windows 11 devices. It is particularly important for business users who deal with sensitive or confidential information.

Key Features:
1. **Full Disk Encryption**: BitLocker encrypts the entire disk, including the operating system, system files, and user data, ensuring that even if the device is lost or stolen, the data remains secure.

2. **Pre-Boot Authentication**: Users must enter a PIN or provide other authentication methods before the computer boots up, adding an extra layer of security.

3. **BitLocker to Go**: This feature extends BitLocker encryption to external USB drives, ensuring data on removable media is also protected.

4. **Recovery Key Management**: BitLocker allows organizations to manage recovery keys centrally, ensuring that in case of password or PIN loss, data can still be recovered.

Windows Information Protection (WIP)

Windows Information Protection is designed to prevent data leakage by protecting sensitive information from being accessed by unauthorized users or applications.

Key Features:
1. **Data Classification**: WIP allows organizations to classify data based on sensitivity, making it easier to apply protection policies.

2. **Encryption and Access Controls**: Sensitive data is encrypted and access is restricted based on policy settings.

3. **Auditing and Reporting**: Organizations can monitor and audit the usage of sensitive data, helping in compliance and incident response.

Credential Guard

Credential Guard is a hardware-based security feature that helps protect against credential theft attacks like Pass-the-Hash. It isolates and secures user credentials from the rest of the system.

Key Features:
1. **Virtualization-Based Security**: Credential Guard uses virtualization-based security to isolate and protect credential information.

2. **Protection Against Pass-the-Hash Attacks**: It prevents attackers from stealing credential hashes and using them to move laterally within a network.

3. **Compatibility**: Credential Guard is compatible with various authentication methods, including smart cards and Windows Hello.

Windows Defender SmartScreen

Windows Defender SmartScreen helps protect against phishing attacks and the download of malicious software. It checks websites and files for potential threats and warns users when they encounter suspicious content.

Key Features:
1. **URL Reputation Checks**: SmartScreen checks the reputation of websites and warns users if they are about to visit a known phishing site.

2. **Download Warnings**: When users attempt to download potentially harmful files, SmartScreen will warn them and advise against proceeding.

These advanced security features, when properly configured and managed, significantly enhance the security posture of Windows 11 in a business environment. Organizations should consider implementing a combination of these features to create a robust security strategy tailored to their specific needs and risk profile. Regular monitoring, updates, and user education are also essential components of any effective security plan.

17.4. Deploying and Managing Windows 11 in an Enterprise Setting

Deploying and managing Windows 11 in an enterprise setting requires a well-thought-out strategy and the use of specialized tools and techniques. This section delves into the key considerations and steps involved in deploying and managing Windows 11 for large organizations.

Key Considerations for Deployment

1. *Assessment and Planning*: Before deploying Windows 11, conduct a thorough assessment of your organization's needs and requirements. Determine the hardware compatibility, software compatibility, and any potential issues that may arise during the deployment process.

2. *Volume Licensing*: Large organizations often opt for volume licensing agreements with Microsoft. This allows for more flexibility in licensing and simplifies the deployment of Windows 11 across multiple devices.

3. *Customized Images*: Create customized Windows 11 images that include necessary applications, configurations, and updates specific to your organization. This ensures consistency across all deployed devices.

4. *Pilot Testing*: Before rolling out Windows 11 to all devices, conduct a pilot test with a small group of users. This helps identify and address any issues that may arise during deployment.

5. *User Training*: Provide training and resources to end-users to help them adapt to Windows 11's new features and interface. A well-informed user base can reduce support requests and increase productivity.

Deployment Tools and Methods

1. *Windows Deployment Services (WDS)*: WDS is a server role in Windows Server that enables network-based installations of Windows operating systems. It allows for remote deployment to multiple devices simultaneously.

2. *System Center Configuration Manager (SCCM)*: SCCM is a comprehensive management solution for deploying and managing Windows 11. It provides features for inventory, software distribution, patch management, and more.

3. *Microsoft Intune*: Intune is a cloud-based service that simplifies mobile device management and ensures compliance with organizational policies. It can also manage Windows 11 devices, including remote wipe and update management.

4. *Windows Autopilot*: Autopilot streamlines the deployment process by allowing users to set up new Windows 11 devices with minimal intervention. It leverages cloud-based configuration and enrollment.

Security and Compliance

1. *Security Baselines*: Implement security baselines provided by Microsoft to ensure that Windows 11 devices are configured securely. Regularly review and update these baselines to adapt to changing threats.

2. *Endpoint Security*: Utilize Windows Defender and Microsoft Defender ATP to protect against malware, advanced threats, and unauthorized access. Configure policies for real-time monitoring and response.

3. *Group Policies*: *Leverage Group Policy to enforce security and compliance settings across Windows 11 devices. Group Policies can control various aspects of the operating system and user behavior.*

Monitoring and Management

1. *Monitoring Tools*: *Use monitoring tools like Microsoft Operations Management Suite (OMS) or Azure Monitor to gain insights into the health and performance of Windows 11 devices in your organization.*

2. *Patch Management*: *Implement a robust patch management strategy to keep Windows 11 devices up to date with the latest security updates and feature releases. This helps protect against vulnerabilities.*

3. *Remote Desktop Services (RDS)*: *RDS allows for remote access and management of Windows 11 devices, which is particularly useful for troubleshooting and support.*

User Experience and Support

1. *Service Desk*: *Establish a service desk or helpdesk to provide technical support and assistance to users. Ensure that support staff are trained in Windows 11 troubleshooting and can address common issues.*

2. *User Feedback*: *Encourage users to provide feedback on their Windows 11 experience. This feedback can be valuable for identifying and resolving issues.*

Compliance and Governance

1. *Compliance Policies*: *Define and enforce compliance policies to ensure that Windows 11 devices adhere to organizational standards and regulatory requirements.*

2. *Data Protection*: *Implement data protection measures, including data encryption and access controls, to safeguard sensitive information on Windows 11 devices.*

Deploying and managing Windows 11 in an enterprise setting is a complex but essential task. With careful planning, the use of appropriate tools, and a focus on security and compliance, organizations can ensure a smooth and secure transition to Windows 11 for their workforce. Regular updates and monitoring are crucial to maintaining a secure and efficient Windows 11 environment.

17.5. Utilizing Enterprise Tools for Management and Security

In an enterprise environment, managing and securing Windows 11 devices is paramount to ensure efficiency, productivity, and data protection. This section explores various enterprise tools and solutions that organizations can utilize for effective management and security.

Enterprise Mobility Management (EMM)

Enterprise Mobility Management solutions are designed to manage and secure mobile devices, including Windows 11 devices. EMM solutions provide features such as device enrollment, policy enforcement, application management, and remote wipe capabilities. Microsoft Intune, part of Microsoft Endpoint Manager, is a prominent EMM solution that offers robust Windows 11 management capabilities in addition to other platforms.

Mobile Device Management (MDM)

MDM solutions focus on managing and securing mobile devices within an organization. For Windows 11 devices, MDM profiles can be used to enforce security policies, configure device settings, and deploy applications remotely. MDM solutions like Microsoft Intune integrate seamlessly with Windows 11 to provide centralized management and security.

Group Policy

Group Policy is a powerful tool for managing Windows 11 devices in an enterprise. It allows administrators to define and enforce policies related to security, system settings, and user configurations. Group Policies can be used to control access, restrict certain actions, and configure device behavior. Group Policy is especially useful for organizations that rely on on-premises Active Directory services.

Windows Autopilot

Windows Autopilot simplifies the provisioning and deployment of new Windows 11 devices in an enterprise setting. It leverages cloud-based configuration and enrollment, reducing the need for manual setup. Administrators can define configuration profiles and settings that are applied automatically during device setup. This streamlines the onboarding process for new employees or devices.

Windows Update for Business

Managing Windows updates is critical for security and stability. Windows Update for Business is an enterprise-grade solution that allows organizations to control the deployment of updates. Administrators can specify maintenance windows, defer updates, and prioritize security patches. This ensures that Windows 11 devices remain up to date while minimizing disruptions to productivity.

Windows Defender Advanced Threat Protection (ATP)

Windows Defender ATP is an endpoint security platform that provides advanced threat protection for Windows 11 devices. It uses machine learning and behavioral analysis to detect and respond to security threats in real-time. Organizations can gain insights into security incidents and take proactive measures to protect sensitive data.

Azure Active Directory (Azure AD)

Azure Active Directory is Microsoft's cloud-based identity and access management solution. It integrates seamlessly with Windows 11, providing secure authentication and access control. Azure AD supports single sign-on (SSO), multi-factor authentication (MFA), and conditional access policies to enhance security.

Security Information and Event Management (SIEM)

SIEM solutions aggregate and analyze security data from various sources, including Windows 11 devices. They provide real-time threat detection, incident response, and compliance reporting. SIEM solutions can help organizations proactively identify and mitigate security risks.

Endpoint Detection and Response (EDR)

EDR solutions focus on detecting and responding to advanced threats and malicious activities on Windows 11 endpoints. They provide visibility into endpoint activities, allowing organizations to investigate and remediate security incidents promptly. Microsoft Defender for Endpoint is an example of an EDR solution.

Compliance and Governance

Enterprise tools often include features for compliance and governance. These tools help organizations adhere to industry regulations and internal policies. They assist in data protection, audit trail management, and reporting to demonstrate compliance.

In conclusion, utilizing enterprise tools for the management and security of Windows 11 devices is essential for organizations of all sizes. These tools enable centralized control, enhance security, and streamline device provisioning and maintenance. By leveraging the right combination of solutions, organizations can create a secure and efficient Windows 11 environment tailored to their specific needs.

Chapter 18: Developer Tools and Resources

18.1. Introduction to Developer Tools in Windows 11

Windows 11 provides an array of developer tools and resources to help software developers create, test, and debug applications efficiently. Whether you're building desktop applications, web applications, or Universal Windows Platform (UWP) apps, Windows 11 offers a comprehensive set of tools to streamline the development process. In this section, we'll introduce you to the key developer tools available in Windows 11.

Visual Studio

Visual Studio is Microsoft's integrated development environment (IDE) that supports a wide range of programming languages, including C#, C++, and JavaScript. It offers a feature-rich code editor, a powerful debugger, and various project templates to kickstart your development projects. Visual Studio provides excellent support for building Windows desktop applications, web applications, mobile apps, and cloud-based solutions.

Visual Studio Code

Visual Studio Code (VS Code) is a lightweight, open-source code editor that has gained immense popularity in the developer community. It's highly customizable and supports numerous programming languages through extensions. VS Code is ideal for web development, cross-platform development, and scripting tasks. It offers an integrated terminal, Git support, and a marketplace with thousands of extensions.

Windows Subsystem for Linux (WSL)

WSL allows developers to run a Linux distribution alongside Windows 11. This is particularly useful for developers who need to work on both Windows and Linux environments. With WSL, you can use command-line tools and utilities from the Linux world without the need for dual-booting or virtual machines. It enhances the development experience for tasks like web development, server administration, and more.

Windows SDK and API

The Windows Software Development Kit (SDK) provides a comprehensive set of libraries, headers, and tools for developing Windows applications. It includes APIs for user interface controls, file system operations, networking, and more. The Windows API is the foundation for building native Windows applications that can take full advantage of the platform's capabilities.

Windows App Certification Kit

When you're ready to distribute your Windows application, the Windows App Certification Kit helps you ensure that it meets Microsoft's quality and performance standards. It performs a series of tests and verifications to identify potential issues and provides guidance on resolving them. This ensures that your app provides a smooth and reliable user experience.

.NET Framework and .NET Core

.NET is a popular framework for building Windows applications. It offers a wide range of libraries and tools for developing desktop applications, web applications, and services. Windows 11 supports both the traditional .NET Framework and the cross-platform .NET Core (now known as .NET 5 and later versions), allowing developers to choose the best framework for their projects.

Windows Template Studio

Windows Template Studio is a Visual Studio extension that simplifies the creation of UWP apps. It provides a wizard-like interface to generate project templates with common layouts and features. This accelerates app development by reducing the initial setup and boilerplate code, allowing developers to focus on their app's unique functionality.

WinDbg

WinDbg is a powerful debugger for Windows applications, kernel-mode drivers, and system-level components. It's an advanced tool used for diagnosing and troubleshooting complex issues, including crash dumps and performance problems. WinDbg is particularly valuable for low-level and system development tasks.

GitHub and Azure DevOps

Microsoft offers developer platforms like GitHub and Azure DevOps, which provide collaboration tools, version control, continuous integration and deployment (CI/CD) pipelines, and project management capabilities. These platforms help developers work efficiently in teams, track code changes, and automate the software delivery process.

In summary, Windows 11 offers a rich ecosystem of developer tools and resources that cater to a wide range of development needs. Whether you're a web developer, a mobile app developer, or working on desktop applications, Windows 11 provides the tools and support to create high-quality software solutions. These tools, combined with the extensive documentation and community resources, empower developers to build innovative applications on the Windows platform.

18.2. Using Visual Studio and Other Development Environments

Developers often rely on integrated development environments (IDEs) to streamline the software development process. In addition to Visual Studio, Windows 11 supports a variety of other development environments that cater to different programming languages and scenarios. Let's explore some of these alternatives and see how they can enhance your development experience.

1. Eclipse

Eclipse is a popular open-source IDE that primarily targets Java development but offers plugins for other languages like C/C++ and Python. It provides a flexible and extensible platform with features like code navigation, refactoring, and debugging. Eclipse's ecosystem includes various plugins and extensions, making it suitable for different development needs.

2. IntelliJ IDEA

IntelliJ IDEA is a robust IDE designed primarily for Java development but also offers support for Kotlin, Groovy, and other JVM-based languages. It's known for its intelligent code assistance, refactoring tools, and deep integration with popular build tools like Gradle and Maven. IntelliJ IDEA provides a community edition with essential features and an ultimate edition with advanced capabilities.

3. PyCharm

PyCharm is JetBrains' IDE specifically tailored for Python development. It offers features like code completion, code analysis, and a powerful debugger for Python developers. PyCharm's professional edition includes additional web development and database tools, making it versatile for full-stack development.

4. Visual Studio Code (VS Code)

While mentioned previously, it's worth highlighting VS Code's popularity among developers. VS Code is a lightweight, highly customizable code editor that supports an extensive range of programming languages through extensions. It's an excellent choice for web development, scripting, and cross-platform development tasks. Its integrated terminal, Git support, and vast extension marketplace make it a versatile tool.

5. NetBeans

NetBeans is another open-source IDE that supports multiple languages, including Java, PHP, and C/C++. It offers features like project management, code templates, and a visual debugger. NetBeans also provides a strong plugin ecosystem to extend its functionality based on your requirements.

6. Android Studio

For Android app development, Android Studio is the official IDE provided by Google. It streamlines the development of Android applications with features like visual layout editors, emulators, and deep integration with the Android platform. Android Studio simplifies the process of creating and deploying Android apps.

7. Xcode

Xcode is Apple's integrated development environment for macOS and iOS app development. It provides tools for building, testing, and debugging apps for Apple's ecosystem, including Swift and Objective-C support. Xcode's Interface Builder simplifies the creation of user interfaces for Apple devices.

8. Web-based IDEs

With the rise of cloud computing, web-based IDEs have gained popularity. Platforms like GitHub Codespaces, Gitpod, and Replit allow developers to code, collaborate, and deploy applications entirely within a web browser. These tools provide the flexibility to work from different devices without the need for local installations.

9. Language-Specific IDEs

Many programming languages have dedicated IDEs that cater specifically to their ecosystems. Examples include RStudio for R programming, RubyMine for Ruby development, and Unity for game development using C#.

10. Command-Line Tools

Some developers prefer to work primarily from the command line, using text editors like Vim or Emacs along with a suite of command-line tools and scripts. This minimalistic approach can be highly efficient for experienced developers and system administrators.

The choice of an IDE or development environment depends on your programming language, project requirements, and personal preferences. Windows 11's versatility ensures compatibility with a wide range of development tools, empowering developers to choose the environment that best suits their needs and expertise. Whether you're developing web applications, mobile apps, or desktop software, Windows 11 provides the flexibility to work with your preferred development tools.

18.3. Developing Apps for Windows 11: A Primer

Developing applications for Windows 11 offers an opportunity to create software that seamlessly integrates with the latest features and capabilities of the operating system. In this section, we'll explore the basics of app development for Windows 11, including the tools, languages, and frameworks commonly used.

1. Programming Languages

Windows 11 supports various programming languages for application development. The most prominent languages include:

- **C#**: C# is a widely used language for Windows app development. It is the primary language for creating Universal Windows Platform (UWP) apps. You can use C# with the .NET framework to build desktop, mobile, and web applications.

- **C++**: C++ is suitable for developing performance-critical applications. Windows 11 offers support for developing native desktop applications using C++ and the Windows API.

- **XAML**: Extensible Application Markup Language (XAML) is a markup language used for designing user interfaces in Windows 11 applications. It works in conjunction with C# or other .NET languages.

- **JavaScript/TypeScript**: For web-based apps, JavaScript and TypeScript are commonly used in conjunction with HTML and CSS. Windows 11 provides tools for building Progressive Web Apps (PWAs) and Electron-based desktop apps using these languages.

- **Python**: Python is gaining popularity for Windows app development, thanks to frameworks like PyQt and Kivy. You can create cross-platform desktop applications using Python.

2. Development Tools

Developers have access to a range of development tools and environments for Windows 11 app development:

- **Visual Studio**: Microsoft's Visual Studio is a comprehensive integrated development environment (IDE) that supports various languages, including C#, C++, and JavaScript/TypeScript. It offers project templates, debugging tools, and a rich set of libraries for Windows app development.

- **Visual Studio Code (VS Code)**: VS Code is a lightweight code editor suitable for various programming languages. It supports extensions that enable Windows 11 app development using different languages and frameworks.

- **Windows App SDK**: Formerly known as the Windows SDK, the Windows App SDK provides libraries and tools for creating UWP apps. It offers APIs for accessing Windows features, such as user interface controls and system services.

- **Electron**: Electron is a framework that allows you to build cross-platform desktop applications using web technologies (HTML, CSS, and JavaScript/TypeScript). It's popular for creating apps like Visual Studio Code and Slack.

- **Qt**: Qt is a cross-platform C++ framework that supports Windows 11 app development. It provides tools for building native-looking applications with a single codebase.

3. Universal Windows Platform (UWP)

UWP is a platform provided by Microsoft for developing Windows 11 applications that run on various Windows devices, such as PCs, tablets, Xbox, and HoloLens. UWP apps can be distributed through the Microsoft Store. They have access to a wide range of APIs for system integration and can be designed to adapt to different screen sizes and input methods.

4. Web Technologies and PWAs

Windows 11 supports Progressive Web Apps (PWAs), which are web applications that can be installed and run like native apps. PWAs use web technologies such as HTML, CSS, and JavaScript/TypeScript and offer offline capabilities, push notifications, and access to device features.

5. Design Guidelines

To create user-friendly and visually appealing Windows 11 apps, developers should follow the design guidelines provided by Microsoft. These guidelines cover aspects such as app layout, typography, color schemes, and navigation patterns.

6. Testing and Debugging

Thorough testing and debugging are essential for delivering high-quality Windows 11 apps. Developers can use tools like the Windows Device Portal, Windows Application Certification Kit, and Visual Studio's debugging features to ensure their apps are stable and perform as expected.

7. Deployment

Once an app is developed and tested, it can be deployed to users through the Microsoft Store, sideloading, or other distribution methods. Microsoft provides resources and documentation on app submission and deployment procedures.

Developing apps for Windows 11 opens up opportunities to reach a broad user base and leverage the latest features of the operating system. Whether you're creating a desktop application, a web-based app, or a cross-platform solution, Windows 11 offers the tools and support needed to bring your ideas to life and deliver valuable software experiences to users.

18.4. Utilizing Windows SDK and API for Custom Development

Windows Software Development Kit (SDK) is a crucial resource for developers aiming to create custom applications that harness the full power of the Windows operating system. In this section, we'll delve into the Windows SDK and explore how to leverage its features and APIs for custom development.

1. What is Windows SDK?

The Windows SDK is a collection of tools, libraries, headers, and documentation provided by Microsoft to assist developers in creating Windows applications. It encompasses various APIs (Application Programming Interfaces) that grant access to Windows features, from low-level system interactions to high-level user interface components.

2. Components of Windows SDK

The Windows SDK includes several components that facilitate different aspects of application development:

- **Headers and Libraries**: These files provide definitions and implementations of functions and data structures used in Windows development. Developers can link against these libraries to access Windows APIs.

- **Debugging Tools**: Windows SDK includes debugging tools like WinDbg, which help developers diagnose and resolve issues in their applications.

- **Documentation**: Comprehensive documentation is provided, which includes guides, reference materials, and sample code to aid developers in understanding and using Windows APIs effectively.

3. Windows API

The Windows API is the core set of functions and interfaces that allow applications to interact with the Windows operating system. It covers a wide range of areas, including file operations, process management, user interface elements, networking, and more.

Developers can use the Windows API to create applications with custom behaviors and functionality not provided by standard libraries or frameworks. This level of customization is especially useful for system utilities, device drivers, and applications that require deep integration with the operating system.

4. Key Concepts and Practices

When utilizing the Windows SDK and API for custom development, developers should keep the following key concepts and practices in mind:

- **Platform Compatibility**: Be aware of the target Windows versions and architectures to ensure your application runs correctly across different systems.

- **Error Handling**: Proper error handling is crucial when working with low-level APIs. Use error codes and messages to diagnose and handle issues gracefully.

- **Security**: Follow security best practices to protect your application and its users. Avoid common vulnerabilities like buffer overflows and injection attacks.

- **Resource Management**: Manage resources such as memory and file handles carefully to prevent leaks and performance degradation.

- **Unicode Support**: Windows APIs often use Unicode for text encoding. Ensure your application handles Unicode characters correctly for internationalization.

- **Threading**: Understand how to work with threads and processes effectively. Windows offers robust support for multithreading, which can improve application performance.

5. Sample Code

Here's a simple example of using the Windows API to create a basic window application in C++:

```cpp
#include <Windows.h>

LRESULT CALLBACK WindowProc(HWND hwnd, UINT uMsg, WPARAM wParam, LPARAM lParam) {
    switch (uMsg) {
        case WM_DESTROY:
            PostQuitMessage(0);
            return 0;
        default:
            return DefWindowProc(hwnd, uMsg, wParam, lParam);
    }
}

int WINAPI WinMain(HINSTANCE hInstance, HINSTANCE hPrevInstance, LPSTR lpCmdLine, int nCmdShow) {
    // Register the window class
    const wchar_t CLASS_NAME[] = L"SampleWindowClass";

    WNDCLASS wc = {0};
    wc.lpfnWndProc = WindowProc;
    wc.hInstance = hInstance;
    wc.lpszClassName = CLASS_NAME;

    RegisterClass(&wc);

    // Create the window
    HWND hwnd = CreateWindowEx(
        0,                              // Optional window styles
        CLASS_NAME,                     // Window class
        L"Sample Window",               // Window title
        WS_OVERLAPPEDWINDOW,            // Window style
        CW_USEDEFAULT, CW_USEDEFAULT,   // Window position
        CW_USEDEFAULT, CW_USEDEFAULT,   // Window size
        NULL,                           // Parent window
        NULL,                           // Menu
        hInstance,                      // Instance handle
        NULL                            // Additional application data
    );
```

```
    if (hwnd == NULL) {
        return 0;
    }

    ShowWindow(hwnd, nCmdShow);

    // Main message loop
    MSG msg = {0};
    while (GetMessage(&msg, NULL, 0, 0)) {
        TranslateMessage(&msg);
        DispatchMessage(&msg);
    }

    return 0;
}
```

This code creates a basic window using the Windows API, which responds to the WM_DESTROY message and exits when the window is closed.

6. Conclusion

Leveraging the Windows SDK and API allows developers to create custom Windows applications with deep integration and unique functionality. Whether you're developing system utilities, specialized tools, or applications that require low-level control, understanding and using the Windows SDK and API effectively is essential for achieving your development goals.

18.5. Best Practices for Software Development on Windows 11

When developing software for Windows 11, adhering to best practices ensures that your applications are robust, secure, and provide a seamless user experience. In this section, we'll explore some key best practices that developers should consider when building software for Windows 11.

1. User-Centered Design

User experience (UX) should be at the forefront of your application design. Consider the following:

- **Modern UI**: Embrace Windows 11's Fluent Design System, which focuses on clarity, content, and adaptability.

- **Responsive Layouts**: Design adaptive layouts that work well on various screen sizes, including tablets and touchscreen devices.

- **Accessibility**: Ensure your app is accessible to users with disabilities by following accessibility guidelines and providing keyboard and screen reader support.

2. Performance Optimization

Optimizing your application for performance is crucial:

- **Resource Efficiency**: Minimize resource usage, such as memory and CPU, to ensure smooth performance.

- **Multithreading**: Utilize multithreading to distribute tasks efficiently and take advantage of multi-core processors.

- **Lazy Loading**: Load resources and data on-demand to reduce startup times.

3. Security

Security should be a top priority:

- **Authentication and Authorization**: Implement robust user authentication and authorization mechanisms to protect user data and prevent unauthorized access.

- **Data Encryption**: Encrypt sensitive data, both in transit and at rest, using encryption standards like TLS and AES.

- **Code Signing**: Digitally sign your application's code to prevent tampering and assure users of its integrity.

4. Compatibility and Updates

Ensure your application remains compatible and up-to-date:

- **Windows Version Support**: Continuously test your app on the latest Windows 11 updates to ensure compatibility.

- **Automatic Updates**: Consider implementing automatic update mechanisms to deliver bug fixes and new features seamlessly.

5. Testing and Quality Assurance

Thorough testing is essential:

- **Cross-Browser and Cross-Platform Testing**: Test your web applications on multiple browsers and operating systems, ensuring compatibility.

- **Unit Testing**: Implement unit tests to verify the correctness of individual components within your application.

- **User Testing**: Conduct user testing to gather feedback and identify usability issues.

6. Documentation and Support

Provide comprehensive documentation and support:

- **User Guides**: Create user-friendly documentation that helps users understand your application's features and functionality.

- **Customer Support**: Offer responsive customer support channels to assist users with inquiries and issues.

7. Performance Monitoring

Monitor your application's performance in real-time:

- **Logging**: Implement logging to record errors, exceptions, and usage data, allowing you to diagnose and resolve issues quickly.

- **Performance Metrics**: Collect and analyze performance metrics to identify bottlenecks and areas for improvement.

8. Scalability and Redundancy

Design your applications for scalability and redundancy:

- **Load Balancing**: Use load balancing to distribute traffic evenly across multiple servers to handle increased loads.

- **Data Backup**: Regularly back up user data and ensure data redundancy to prevent data loss.

9. Licensing and Piracy Prevention

Protect your intellectual property and revenue:

- **Licensing Models**: Implement licensing models that suit your application, such as one-time purchases, subscriptions, or freemium.

- **Anti-Piracy Measures**: Incorporate anti-piracy measures to deter unauthorized distribution and use of your software.

10. Community Engagement

Engage with your user community:

- **Feedback Mechanisms**: Provide avenues for users to submit feedback and feature requests.

- **Beta Testing**: Consider involving users in beta testing to gather real-world feedback.

By following these best practices, you can develop high-quality software for Windows 11 that meets user expectations and stands out in the competitive software landscape.

Remember that continuous improvement and adaptation to evolving technology trends are key to the long-term success of your applications.

19.1. The Roadmap for Windows 11: What's Next?

As an operating system that continually evolves, Windows 11 always has its sights set on the future. In this section, we'll delve into what's on the horizon for Windows 11, examining the roadmap and upcoming features that users can anticipate in the next updates and releases.

1. Feature Updates

Windows 11 follows a regular update schedule, with major feature updates being rolled out semi-annually. These updates often bring new features, enhancements, and improvements to the operating system. Users can expect features that focus on user experience, productivity, security, and more.

2. User Interface Enhancements

Microsoft continues to refine and improve the Windows 11 user interface (UI). Expect changes to the Start Menu, taskbar, and system icons. Microsoft is known for adopting user feedback, so you may see adjustments based on user input.

3. Gaming and DirectX

With the growing popularity of gaming on Windows, updates related to gaming performance and features are likely. DirectX, Microsoft's gaming technology, is also expected to receive updates, providing developers with new tools and gamers with improved performance.

4. Security and Privacy

Enhanced security features are a priority for Windows 11. Look out for improvements in Windows Defender, User Account Control (UAC), and privacy settings. Microsoft continually addresses emerging threats to keep users safe.

5. Cortana and Voice Control

Cortana, Microsoft's virtual assistant, is likely to receive updates, making it more intelligent and user-friendly. Voice control and AI-powered features are expected to be integrated more deeply into the operating system.

B. Upcoming Features and Enhancements

While the specific features in each update remain a surprise until their official announcement, some general areas of improvement can be expected:

1. Cloud Integration

As cloud computing becomes increasingly important, Windows 11 will likely offer tighter integration with cloud services. This may include more seamless synchronization of settings, files, and data across devices.

2. AI and Machine Learning

Microsoft is heavily investing in AI and machine learning. Future updates may include AI-powered features that enhance user productivity, assist with content creation, and improve search and recommendations.

3. Accessibility

Windows 11 is committed to accessibility. Expect further enhancements to assist users with disabilities, including improvements to Narrator, Magnifier, and other accessibility features.

4. Developer-Focused Updates

For developers, Windows 11 updates often come with new APIs, tools, and features. This can facilitate the development of innovative applications that leverage the latest technologies.

C. The Role of the Windows Insider Program

The Windows Insider Program allows enthusiasts and developers to test early builds of Windows 11. Microsoft values feedback from insiders, and their input helps shape the final release of updates. Joining the Insider Program is an opportunity to get a sneak peek at upcoming features and contribute to their development.

D. Staying Informed

To stay informed about upcoming Windows 11 features and updates, regularly check Microsoft's official announcements and blogs. These sources provide detailed information about what to expect in the next updates and how to prepare for them.

In conclusion, Windows 11's roadmap is filled with exciting possibilities. With each update, Microsoft aims to enhance the user experience, boost productivity, and bolster security. Staying up-to-date with the latest features ensures that you can make the most of your Windows 11 experience while benefiting from the latest innovations and improvements.

19.2. Upcoming Features and Enhancements in Windows 11

As Windows 11 continues to evolve, users can look forward to a range of upcoming features and enhancements designed to improve their computing experience. While

Microsoft releases updates on a regular basis, it's essential to have a sense of what's on the horizon to make the most of your Windows 11 device.

Here are some anticipated features and enhancements you can expect in future Windows 11 updates:

1. UI Enhancements

Microsoft is committed to refining the user interface (UI) of Windows 11 based on user feedback. This means you can anticipate changes to the Start Menu, taskbar, and system icons. The goal is to make the interface more intuitive and visually appealing.

2. Performance Boosts

Performance improvements are always a priority. Upcoming updates may focus on optimizing the operating system for better speed and responsiveness. This is particularly important for users who rely on Windows 11 for resource-intensive tasks, such as gaming and content creation.

3. Integration with Cloud Services

As cloud computing becomes increasingly central to the digital landscape, Windows 11 is likely to offer deeper integration with cloud services. This could result in more seamless synchronization of settings, files, and data across devices. It also means that users can access their data from anywhere with an internet connection.

4. Gaming Enhancements

Given the popularity of gaming on Windows, expect updates related to gaming performance and features. Microsoft is continually working to improve gaming experiences, which may include DirectX updates, new gaming modes, and enhancements to the Xbox app.

5. Security and Privacy

Microsoft is dedicated to enhancing the security and privacy of Windows 11. Look out for updates to Windows Defender, User Account Control (UAC), and privacy settings. These updates will help safeguard your data and protect your system from emerging threats.

6. Accessibility Improvements

Accessibility is a crucial aspect of Windows 11's development. Upcoming updates may include further enhancements to assist users with disabilities. This could involve improvements to Narrator, Magnifier, and other accessibility features, making the operating system more inclusive for all users.

7. AI and Machine Learning Integration

Microsoft's investment in artificial intelligence (AI) and machine learning is evident in Windows 11's development. Future updates may incorporate AI-powered features that enhance user productivity, assist with content creation, and improve search and recommendations.

8. Developer-Focused Updates

Developers can also look forward to updates that cater to their needs. These updates may introduce new APIs, tools, and features to facilitate the development of innovative applications that leverage the latest technologies.

9. Bug Fixes and Quality Improvements

In addition to introducing new features, Microsoft is committed to resolving existing issues and improving the overall quality of the operating system. Updates often include bug fixes and stability enhancements to ensure a smoother user experience.

10. Insider Program Participation

If you're eager to get a sneak peek at upcoming features and actively contribute to their development, consider joining the Windows Insider Program. Insiders have the opportunity to test early builds of Windows 11, providing valuable feedback that helps shape the final release of updates.

11. Staying Informed

To stay informed about the latest features and updates coming to Windows 11, regularly check Microsoft's official announcements, blogs, and the Windows Update settings on your device. Staying informed ensures that you can take full advantage of the improvements and innovations that each update brings.

In conclusion, the future of Windows 11 is filled with exciting possibilities. With each update, Microsoft aims to enhance the user experience, boost performance, and bolster security. Keeping an eye on upcoming features and enhancements allows you to stay ahead of the curve and make the most of your Windows 11 device.

19.3. Participating in the Windows Insider Program

The Windows Insider Program is a valuable initiative for users who want to get involved in shaping the future of Windows 11. By participating in this program, you gain access to early preview builds of the operating system, providing you with a glimpse of upcoming features and improvements before they are released to the general public. In this section, we'll explore the Windows Insider Program, how to join, and what you can expect as a participant.

1. What is the Windows Insider Program?

The Windows Insider Program is a community of tech enthusiasts, developers, and Windows enthusiasts who collaborate with Microsoft to test pre-release versions of Windows. These pre-release versions, also known as "Insider builds," allow participants to explore new features, provide feedback, and help identify and report issues. This feedback is invaluable to Microsoft as it helps them refine Windows 11 and prioritize feature development and bug fixes.

2. Why Join the Windows Insider Program?

There are several compelling reasons to become a Windows Insider:

- **Early Access:** Insiders get early access to upcoming features and improvements, allowing them to be among the first to experience what's new in Windows 11.

- **Influence the Future:** As an Insider, your feedback directly influences the development of Windows 11. Microsoft values user input and often makes changes based on user suggestions and bug reports.

- **Learn and Explore:** Participating in the program provides a learning opportunity. You can explore new features, test compatibility with your software and hardware, and gain a deeper understanding of the Windows operating system.

3. How to Join the Windows Insider Program

Joining the Windows Insider Program is straightforward:

Step 1: Sign In with a Microsoft Account

Ensure that you're signed in to Windows 11 with a Microsoft account. If you don't have one, you can create it during the setup process.

Step 2: Open Settings

Click on the Start button and then click on the "Settings" gear icon. Alternatively, you can press Win + I to open Settings.

Step 3: Access Windows Insider Program Settings

In the Settings window, click on "Windows Update" in the left sidebar. Then, click on the "Windows Insider Program" tab on the right.

Step 4: Enroll in the Program

Click on the "Get Started" button. Follow the on-screen instructions to enroll in the Windows Insider Program.

When enrolling, you'll be prompted to choose an Insider channel. There are three channels to choose from:

- **Dev Channel:** This channel provides the earliest access to new features, but it may contain more bugs and stability issues.

- **Beta Channel:** The Beta channel offers a balance between early access and stability. It's a good choice for most enthusiasts.

- **Release Preview Channel:** This channel provides access to updates that are close to being released to the general public and is the most stable option.

Choose the channel that best suits your preferences.

Step 6: Download and Install Insider Builds

Once you've enrolled and chosen a channel, Windows Update will download and install the corresponding Insider builds on your device. You'll receive these updates as part of your regular Windows Update process.

4. Providing Feedback

As an Insider, you're encouraged to provide feedback through the Feedback Hub app. This app allows you to submit feedback, bug reports, and feature suggestions directly to Microsoft. Your feedback helps shape the development of Windows 11 and improve its overall quality.

5. Precautions for Insiders

While participating in the Windows Insider Program can be exciting, it's essential to keep a few things in mind:

- **Expect Bugs:** Insider builds may contain bugs and compatibility issues. Be prepared to encounter occasional glitches, and consider using a secondary device for testing if your primary device requires stability.

- **Data Backup:** Back up your important data regularly, as Insider builds can sometimes lead to unexpected data loss.

- **Privacy:** Be aware that Insider builds may collect diagnostic data and usage information. Review and adjust your privacy settings as needed.

6. Leaving the Windows Insider Program

If you decide to leave the Windows Insider Program, you can do so at any time by following these steps:

1. Open Settings.
2. Go to "Windows Update" > "Windows Insider Program."

3. Click on "Stop Insider Preview builds."
4. Follow the on-screen instructions to stop receiving Insider builds.

7. Conclusion

Participating in the Windows Insider Program is a rewarding experience for users who want to be at the forefront of Windows 11 development. It provides an opportunity to explore upcoming features, contribute to the development process, and influence the direction of Windows. However, it's essential to approach it with awareness of potential issues and to provide constructive feedback to help Microsoft refine its operating system.

19.4. The Role of Community Feedback in Shaping Windows

Community feedback plays a pivotal role in the development and evolution of the Windows operating system. Microsoft has a long history of engaging with its user community to gather insights, address issues, and prioritize new features. In this section, we'll delve into how community feedback contributes to shaping Windows and how you can get involved in this collaborative process.

1. A History of User Feedback

Microsoft's commitment to user feedback can be traced back to the Windows Insider Program, which was launched with Windows 10 and continued with Windows 11. This program allows enthusiasts, developers, and everyday users to test early builds of Windows, report issues, and suggest improvements.

Over the years, the Windows Insider Program has grown into a thriving community of millions of members worldwide. Participants are encouraged to share their thoughts, report bugs, and make feature requests, effectively becoming co-creators of the Windows experience.

2. Feedback Channels

Microsoft provides various channels through which users can submit feedback and engage with the development team:

- **Feedback Hub:** The Feedback Hub app, integrated into Windows, serves as the primary platform for submitting feedback. Users can provide details about issues they encounter, suggest enhancements, and upvote feedback from others.

- **UserVoice:** Microsoft also utilizes UserVoice, a web-based platform, for collecting and prioritizing user suggestions. Users can submit ideas, view other suggestions, and vote on the ones they find most valuable.

- **Forums and Social Media:** Microsoft maintains forums and social media channels where users can discuss Windows features and issues. These platforms provide additional avenues for feedback and community engagement.

3. How Feedback Shapes Windows

User feedback has a direct impact on the development of Windows in several ways:

- **Bug Fixes:** Reports of software bugs and issues are taken seriously. Microsoft's development team investigates these reports and works to resolve them in subsequent updates.

- **Feature Development:** User suggestions and feature requests are evaluated and considered for inclusion in future Windows updates. Some of the most popular and requested features have been added based on community feedback.

- **Quality Improvements:** User feedback contributes to enhancing the overall quality and stability of Windows. It helps identify and address issues that might not have been apparent during internal testing.

- **Prioritization:** The volume and significance of feedback help Microsoft prioritize development efforts. High-impact issues and popular feature requests are more likely to receive attention.

4. How to Provide Effective Feedback

When providing feedback to shape Windows, consider the following tips to make your input more effective:

- **Be Specific:** Clearly describe the issue or suggestion, including the steps to reproduce a problem. Specific details make it easier for developers to understand and address the issue.

- **Check for Duplicates:** Before submitting feedback, search for similar reports to avoid duplicating entries. Upvoting existing feedback can also help highlight important issues.

- **Use the Right Category:** Select the appropriate category and subcategory when submitting feedback. This helps direct your feedback to the relevant teams.

- **Be Constructive:** When reporting issues, focus on providing constructive feedback. Explain why a particular feature or change is important and how it would benefit users.

- **Participate in Discussions:** Engage with other users in discussions about feedback. Your insights and experiences can complement and strengthen the feedback provided by the community.

- **Stay Informed:** Follow Microsoft's official communications to stay informed about updates, changes, and responses to feedback. This can help you understand the status of your feedback.

5. The Impact of Community Collaboration

The collaborative efforts of the Windows community, including Insiders, enthusiasts, and users, have significantly influenced the direction of Windows 11. Many user-driven improvements and refinements have been made, making Windows a more user-friendly and feature-rich operating system.

Microsoft continues to value and prioritize user feedback as it evolves Windows. By actively participating in feedback channels, you can play a vital role in shaping the future of the operating system and ensuring it meets the needs of its diverse user base. Your contributions, whether reporting issues or suggesting new features, help create a better Windows experience for everyone.

19.5. Predicting Future Trends in Windows Operating Systems

As Windows 11 continues to evolve and adapt to the changing landscape of technology, it's essential to look ahead and consider the potential trends and developments that may shape the future of Windows operating systems. While we cannot predict the future with certainty, we can identify some areas of interest and innovation that may influence the direction of Windows in the coming years.

1. Enhanced Integration with Cloud Services

One of the prominent trends in the tech industry is the increased reliance on cloud computing and services. Windows operating systems are likely to further integrate with cloud platforms, enabling seamless synchronization of settings, applications, and data across devices. This integration may enhance mobility and accessibility, allowing users to access their Windows environment from virtually anywhere.

2. Emphasis on Security and Privacy

As cyber threats continue to evolve, Windows is expected to place an even greater emphasis on security and privacy features. This includes advanced threat detection, encryption, and user-centric privacy controls. Protecting user data and maintaining a secure computing environment will remain a top priority.

3. Artificial Intelligence and Machine Learning Integration

AI and machine learning technologies are poised to play a more significant role in Windows operating systems. These technologies can enhance user experiences by providing personalized recommendations, optimizing system performance, and automating routine tasks. Voice recognition, natural language processing, and intelligent virtual assistants may become more integral to the Windows experience.

4. Continued User Interface Evolution

The user interface (UI) of Windows is likely to continue evolving to accommodate new form factors and devices. Adaptive UIs that seamlessly transition between different modes (e.g., desktop, tablet, and mobile) may become more prevalent. Touch and gesture-based interactions may also see further improvements.

5. Inclusive and Accessibility Features

Accessibility remains a crucial aspect of Windows development. Future versions may continue to introduce innovative accessibility features to make the operating system more inclusive for users with disabilities. This includes improved screen readers, voice commands, and other assistive technologies.

6. Cross-Platform Compatibility

Microsoft has been working towards a more unified ecosystem, allowing users to switch seamlessly between Windows, Xbox, and other Microsoft devices. This trend is expected to continue, providing users with a cohesive experience across various platforms.

7. Sustainable Computing

Sustainability is gaining importance in the tech industry. Future Windows versions may incorporate features and optimizations to reduce energy consumption and promote environmentally friendly computing practices.

8. Evolving App Ecosystem

The Windows app ecosystem is likely to continue evolving, with more apps adopting modern design principles and utilizing the latest technologies. The Microsoft Store may see improvements in curation, making it easier for users to discover high-quality apps.

9. Edge Computing and Local AI

Edge computing, where data processing occurs closer to the data source, may become more prevalent in Windows. This can lead to faster and more efficient data processing, particularly in scenarios involving IoT devices.

10. User-Generated Content and Collaboration

Windows may further embrace user-generated content and collaboration tools. Enhanced support for content creation, sharing, and collaboration can empower users to be more productive and creative within the operating system.

While these trends provide a glimpse into the potential future of Windows operating systems, it's essential to remember that the development of such complex software is influenced by various factors, including technological advancements, user feedback, and market demands. As users and technology enthusiasts, staying informed and actively participating in the Windows Insider Program and other feedback channels can contribute to the ongoing evolution of Windows and ensure that it continues to meet the needs and expectations of its diverse user base.

20.1. Key Takeaways from the Windows 11 Journey

As we reach the final chapter of this comprehensive guide to Windows 11, it's time to reflect on the key takeaways and insights gained throughout the journey. Windows 11 is a modern and user-friendly operating system that offers a wide range of features and functionalities to enhance your computing experience. In this concluding section, we'll summarize the essential points covered in this guide and provide you with a concise overview of what you've learned.

1. Windows 11 Evolution: A New Era

You've explored the evolution of Windows operating systems and witnessed the significant changes introduced in Windows 11. From the redesigned Start Menu to enhanced performance and security features, Windows 11 represents a new era in the world of computing.

2. Personalization and Customization

Windows 11 empowers you to personalize your computing environment like never before. You've learned how to customize the desktop, choose themes, and configure settings to tailor your Windows experience to your preferences.

3. Productivity and Collaboration

Windows 11 is equipped with a suite of productivity tools, including Microsoft Office integration, Outlook for email management, OneNote for note-taking, and Teams for collaboration. These tools can streamline your work and help you stay organized.

4. Multimedia and Entertainment

Discover how to enjoy multimedia and entertainment on Windows 11, whether it's playing music and videos, editing photos and videos, or exploring gaming features through Xbox integration.

5. Networking and Connectivity

Learn how to set up and manage network connections, share files and folders, and troubleshoot common network issues. Remote access and VPN usage have also been covered.

6. Advanced Customization and Tweaks

For power users and enthusiasts, Windows 11 offers advanced customization options. You've explored the Windows Registry, customized the Taskbar and Start Menu, optimized graphic settings, and managed power settings.

7. Command Line and PowerShell Mastery

Master the command-line interface with Command Prompt and PowerShell. You've learned basic and advanced commands, automation with batch files and scripts, and how to manage system resources and services.

8. Security and Maintenance

Understand the importance of security and maintenance in Windows 11. You've explored Windows Updates, security tools like Windows Defender, system maintenance, user account control, and system restore.

9. Troubleshooting Common Issues

Equip yourself with troubleshooting skills to diagnose and resolve hardware, software, network, display, and advanced issues effectively. Troubleshooting is a crucial skill for maintaining a healthy Windows environment.

10. Accessibility Features

Explore the accessibility features in Windows 11 and how to customize visual, audio, and input settings for accessibility. Learn about Narrator, Magnifier, and Speech Recognition to create an inclusive computing environment.

11. Virtualization and Managing Multiple Environments

Discover the world of virtualization in Windows 11. You've learned about Windows Subsystem for Linux (WSL), managing virtual machines with Hyper-V, and best practices for running multiple operating systems.

12. Integrating with Mobile Devices

Windows 11 integrates seamlessly with mobile devices. You've explored features like linking your phone, managing notifications, using Your Phone app, synchronizing files and settings, and remote device management.

13. Exploring Advanced Features

Delve into advanced features like widgets, touchpad gestures, spatial sound, AI and machine learning integration, and professional graphic features.

14. Customizing for Business and Enterprise

For business users, this guide has covered topics related to Windows 11 in the business environment, including group policies, advanced security, deployment, and enterprise management tools.

15. Developer Tools and Resources

Introduction to developer tools in Windows 11, using Visual Studio, developing apps, utilizing Windows SDK and API for custom development, and best practices for software development.

16. Future of Windows: Upcoming Features and Updates

Gain insights into the potential future of Windows operating systems, including trends such as enhanced cloud integration, improved security, AI integration, and continued user interface evolution.

17. Conclusion: Embracing the Full Potential of Windows 11

As you conclude this guide, remember that Windows 11 offers a vast array of features and possibilities. Embrace what you've learned to create a personalized and efficient Windows 11 experience. Stay updated with new changes, continue learning, and make the most of the resources available to become a Windows 11 expert.

The journey doesn't end here; it's just the beginning of your mastery of Windows 11. Whether you're a casual user, a business professional, or a developer, Windows 11 has something to offer, and your understanding of this versatile operating system will continue to grow as you explore its endless possibilities.

20.2. Resources for Continued Learning and Support

As you've completed your journey through this comprehensive guide to Windows 11, it's essential to acknowledge that technology, especially operating systems, is constantly evolving. Staying up-to-date with the latest developments, mastering new features, and troubleshooting emerging issues are crucial for maintaining a smooth and efficient Windows 11 experience. In this section, we'll explore various resources and avenues for your continued learning and support needs.

1. Microsoft Documentation and Official Resources

Microsoft's official website and documentation are valuable sources of information. You can access detailed guides, tutorials, and FAQs related to Windows 11. The Microsoft Support page offers solutions to common problems, updates, and troubleshooting guides.

2. Online Forums and Communities

Online communities and forums can be incredibly helpful when you encounter issues or have questions about Windows 11. Websites like Microsoft Community and Ten Forums have active communities where users discuss problems and solutions. Engaging with these communities can provide practical insights and solutions.

3. YouTube Tutorials and Video Content

YouTube is a treasure trove of Windows 11 tutorials and guides. Many tech enthusiasts and professionals create video content to walk you through various aspects of the operating system. You can find videos on topics ranging from customization tips to advanced troubleshooting.

4. Technology News Websites

Stay informed about the latest Windows 11 updates, features, and trends by following technology news websites like The Verge, Ars Technica, and Windows Central. These websites often publish in-depth articles and reviews.

5. Books and eBooks

Consider exploring books and eBooks dedicated to Windows 11. Many authors and publishers release comprehensive guides and reference materials that can deepen your knowledge. Look for titles on popular online bookstores or libraries.

6. Online Courses and Training

Several online platforms offer courses and training related to Windows 11. Websites like LinkedIn Learning, Udemy, and Coursera provide courses on Windows 11 administration, security, and more.

7. Windows Insider Program

If you enjoy being at the forefront of technology, consider joining the Windows Insider Program. This program allows you to test upcoming Windows features and provide feedback directly to Microsoft.

8. Professional Support

For business users and enterprises, Microsoft offers professional support plans. These plans provide access to dedicated support personnel who can assist with complex issues and ensure business continuity.

9. Local User Groups and Workshops

Explore local user groups or workshops related to Windows and technology in your area. These events can be a great way to network with fellow enthusiasts, share knowledge, and learn from experts.

10. Experimentation and Exploration

One of the best ways to learn is by hands-on experience. Don't hesitate to explore Windows 11 on your own, experiment with settings, and try out new features. Just remember to back up your data and be cautious when making significant changes.

Remember that the technology landscape is continually evolving, and Windows 11 will receive updates and improvements over time. Embrace the learning process, adapt to changes, and make the most of the resources available to you. By staying informed and engaged, you can make the most of your Windows 11 experience and harness its full potential.

20.3. Building a Personalized and Efficient Windows 11 Experience

As you conclude your journey through this comprehensive guide to Windows 11, it's crucial to reflect on how to build and maintain a personalized and efficient Windows 11 experience. While you've learned about the operating system's features, tools, and customization options, this section will offer insights into tailoring your Windows 11 environment to suit your specific needs and preferences.

1. Customizing the Start Menu and Taskbar

The Start Menu and Taskbar are central to your Windows 11 experience. Take some time to arrange and customize these elements to make navigation more efficient. You can pin your most-used apps, organize them into folders, and adjust the Taskbar's position to suit your workflow.

2. Personalizing Your Desktop

Windows 11 allows you to personalize your desktop with various themes, backgrounds, and accent colors. Experiment with different combinations to create a visual environment that you find pleasing and conducive to productivity.

```
To change your desktop background:
1. Right-click on the desktop.
2. Select "Personalize."
3. Choose a background image or slideshow.
4. Adjust other visual settings to your liking.
```

3. Organizing Files and Folders

Maintaining a well-organized file and folder structure is essential for efficient workflow. Regularly organize and categorize your files, and consider using descriptive file names. Utilize the built-in libraries and folders, such as Documents, Pictures, and Downloads, to keep related files together.

4. Embracing Keyboard Shortcuts

Keyboard shortcuts can significantly enhance your productivity. Windows 11 offers a range of keyboard shortcuts for various tasks. Learning and using these shortcuts can save you time and reduce reliance on the mouse.

```
Press Win + D to show or hide the desktop.
Press Alt + Tab to switch between open applications.
Press Win + L to lock your computer.
Press Ctrl + Shift + Esc to open Task Manager.
```

5. Managing Notifications

Customize your notification settings to avoid distractions and stay focused. You can choose which apps are allowed to send notifications and adjust their priority.

```
To manage notifications:
1. Go to Settings > System > Notifications.
2. Customize notification settings for each app.
```

6. Regular Maintenance and Updates

To ensure your Windows 11 system remains efficient and secure, regularly install updates and perform system maintenance tasks. Keep your drivers, apps, and the operating system up to date.

```
To check for updates:
1. Go to Settings > Windows Update.
2. Click on "Check for updates."
3. Install any available updates.
```

7. Backup and Data Security

Protect your data by setting up regular backups. Windows 11 includes features like File History and OneDrive for this purpose. Additionally, consider using a reputable antivirus software for enhanced security.

8. Exploring Additional Software

While Windows 11 comes with a variety of built-in apps and tools, you may need additional software for specific tasks or preferences. Explore the Microsoft Store or other trusted sources for applications that can complement your workflow.

9. Adapting to Changes

Technology evolves, and so does Windows 11. Be open to embracing new features and changes that Microsoft introduces through updates. Learning how to adapt to these changes will help you stay efficient and up-to-date.

10. Seeking Help and Community Support

If you encounter challenges or have questions, don't hesitate to seek help from online communities, forums, or Microsoft's official support channels. Often, others have faced similar issues and can provide guidance.

Remember that Windows 11 is a versatile platform that can be tailored to suit your unique needs and preferences. By following these tips and exploring the possibilities, you can create a personalized and efficient Windows 11 experience that enhances your productivity and enjoyment of this operating system.

20.4. Staying Updated and Adapting to New Changes

As you wrap up your journey mastering Windows 11, it's important to emphasize the significance of staying updated and adapting to new changes within the operating system. Microsoft continuously evolves and enhances Windows 11 through regular updates, bug fixes, and feature additions. In this final section, we'll explore strategies for staying current with Windows 11 updates and embracing future changes.

1. Enabling Automatic Updates

One of the simplest ways to ensure your Windows 11 system remains up to date is by enabling automatic updates. By default, Windows 11 is set to download and install updates automatically. However, it's advisable to double-check and confirm this setting:

```
To check automatic update settings:
1. Go to Settings > Windows Update.
2. Click on "Advanced options."
3. Ensure that "Automatically download updates" is turned on.
```

2. Join the Windows Insider Program

For those who want to get early access to upcoming features and provide feedback to Microsoft, consider joining the Windows Insider Program. This program allows you to test pre-release versions of Windows 11 and be part of shaping its future.

```
To join the Windows Insider Program:
1. Go to Settings > Windows Update.
2. Click on "Windows Insider Program" in the left sidebar.
3. Follow the prompts to enroll and select your preferred update channel.
```

3. Regularly Check for Updates

Even with automatic updates enabled, it's a good practice to manually check for updates from time to time. This ensures that critical updates are installed promptly.

```
To manually check for updates:
1. Go to Settings > Windows Update.
2. Click on "Check for updates."
3. Install any available updates.
```

4. Be Open to Change

As Microsoft introduces new features and interface changes, be open to adapting your workflow. While change can be intimidating, it often brings improvements and optimizations that can enhance your experience.

5. Explore New Features

With each major update, Windows 11 may introduce new features and improvements. Take the time to explore these additions, as they may offer valuable tools that can boost your productivity.

6. Keep an Eye on Community Feedback

Many Windows 11 users share their experiences and feedback on online forums and communities. Monitoring these discussions can provide insights into common issues, workarounds, and tips for optimizing your Windows 11 experience.

7. Stay Informed

Stay informed about upcoming updates and changes by following official Microsoft blogs and announcements. This will keep you ahead of the curve and prepared for what's next in Windows 11.

8. Backup Your Data

Before major updates, it's a good practice to back up your important data. While rare, updates can sometimes result in unexpected issues, and having a backup ensures you won't lose valuable information.

In conclusion, mastering Windows 11 is an ongoing journey. By enabling automatic updates, staying informed, and being open to change, you can ensure that you're always using the latest and most efficient version of Windows 11. Embrace updates as opportunities for improvement, and continue to explore and adapt to the evolving features of this powerful operating system.

20.5. Final Thoughts: Embracing the Full Potential of Windows 11

As we conclude this comprehensive guide to mastering Windows 11, it's essential to reflect on the journey you've undertaken and the full potential of this powerful operating system. Windows 11 is more than just a platform for getting work done; it's a versatile ecosystem that can adapt to your needs and preferences. In this final section, we'll delve into some closing thoughts to help you make the most of Windows 11.

1. Personalization and Productivity

Windows 11 offers extensive personalization options, allowing you to tailor your desktop, start menu, and overall user experience. Don't hesitate to experiment with themes, backgrounds, and layouts to create a workspace that inspires productivity and suits your style.

2. Integration with Microsoft Services

Leverage the integration of Windows 11 with Microsoft services like OneDrive, Office 365, and Teams. This integration fosters seamless collaboration, efficient document management, and simplified communication within your digital ecosystem.

3. Security and Privacy

Prioritize security and privacy by regularly updating your system, using built-in security features, and being cautious about the apps and services you install. Windows 11 provides robust security measures, but your proactive approach is invaluable.

4. Staying Organized

Utilize tools like Task View, Snap Layouts, and virtual desktops to stay organized and manage multiple tasks efficiently. Windows 11's user-friendly interface is designed to help you streamline your workflow.

5. Embracing New Features

Be open to embracing new features and technologies introduced in Windows 11. Features like Widgets, Snap Layouts, and improved touch and pen input can enhance your productivity and make daily tasks more enjoyable.

6. Continuous Learning

Technology evolves, and so does Windows 11. Keep the spirit of continuous learning alive. Explore online resources, forums, and communities to stay updated on tips, tricks, and hidden gems within the operating system.

7. Support and Community

Remember that you're not alone in your Windows 11 journey. Communities and support channels are available for troubleshooting, sharing experiences, and seeking assistance. Microsoft's official support resources are a valuable asset.

8. Adaptability and Growth

Lastly, Windows 11's adaptability makes it suitable for a wide range of users, from professionals and creatives to gamers and students. Embrace this adaptability, and allow Windows 11 to grow with you as your needs change.

In closing, Windows 11 is a dynamic and evolving platform that can empower you in various aspects of your digital life. By personalizing your experience, staying secure, and embracing new features, you can unlock the full potential of Windows 11. Continuously learning and adapting ensures that you'll make the most of this innovative operating system. Whether you're a newcomer or a seasoned Windows user, Windows 11 offers exciting opportunities for productivity, creativity, and exploration. Enjoy your Windows 11 journey to the fullest!

www.ingramcontent.com/pod-product-compliance
Lightning Source LLC
La Vergne TN
LVHW051324050326
832903LV00031B/3354

* 9 7 9 8 8 7 7 8 6 4 4 3 6 *